The Big Book of MONSTERS!

The Big Book of MONSTERS!

Jokes and Facts and Games and Stories about Monsters and Witches and Ghouls!

Written and compiled by Guy Campbell & Mark Devins
Illustrated by Paul Moran

Gramercy Books
New York

Originally published as three volumes by Egmont Books Limited under the titles:
The World's Funniest Monster Jokes for Kids
copyright © 2003 Egmont Books Limited

The World's Most Amazing Monster Facts for Kids
copyright © 2003 Egmont Books Limited

The World's Scariest Monster Games and Stories for Kids
copyright © 2003 Egmont Books Limited

This 2004 edition is published by Gramercy Books, an imprint of Random House Value Publishing, a division of Random House, Inc., New York, by arrangement with Egmont Books Limited.

Gramercy is a registered trademark and the colophon is a trademark of Random House, Inc.

Random House
New York • Toronto • London • Sydney • Auckland
www.randomhouse.com

Printed and bound in the U.A.E

A catalog record for this title is available from the Library of Congress.

ISBN 0-517-22457-7

10 9 8 7 6 5 4 3 2 1

CONTENTS

PART 1

MONSTER JOKES

CONTENTS

PART 2
MONSTER FACTS

CONTENTS

PART 3

MONSTER GAMES & STORIES

PART 1

MONSTER JOKES

DEAD FUNNY!

Jokes from Beyond the Grave

Why don't skeletons play music in church?
They have no organs!

Why didn't the skeleton dance at the Halloween party?
It had no body to dance with!

Why are graveyards so noisy?
Because of all the coffin!

What did the skeleton say to the bartender?
Bring me three beers and a mop!

What did the skeleton say while riding his Harley Davidson motorbike?
I'm bone to be wild!

How can you tell if a corpse is angry?
It flips its lid!

Where do undertakers go to gamble?
Hearse races!

Why are skeletons usually so calm?
Nothing gets under their skin!

When can't you bury people who live opposite a graveyard?
When they're not dead!

Who was the most famous French skeleton?
Napoleon bone-apart!

What instrument do skeletons play?
Trom-bone!

What do you call a skeleton who won't get up in the mornings?
Lazy bones!

Two men were walking home after a Halloween party and decided to take a shortcut through the cemetery. Right in the middle of the cemetery they were startled by a tap-tap-tapping noise coming from the shadows. Trembling with fear, they found an old man with a hammer and chisel, chipping away at one of the headstones.

"Holy cow, Mister," one of them said, after catching his breath, "You scared us half to death – we thought you were a ghost! What are you doing working here so late at night?"

"Those fools!" the old man grumbled. "They spelled my name wrong!"

Why wasn't the naughty skeleton afraid of the police?

Because he knew they couldn't pin anything on him!

What happened to the boat that sank in the sea full of piranha fish?
It came back with a skeleton crew!

Who won the skeleton beauty contest?
No body!

When does a skeleton laugh?
When something tickles his funny bone!

What did the skeleton say when his brother told a lie?
You can't fool me, I can see right through you!

Who was the most famous skeleton detective?
Sherlock Bones!

Why didn't the skeleton eat the cafeteria food?
Because he didn't have the stomach for it!

Why couldn't the skeleton cross the road?
He didn't have the guts!

How do skeletons call their friends?
On the telebone!

The teacher asked the class to write about an unusual event that happened during the past week. Little Johnny got up and read his essay.
It began, "Daddy fell into the well last week ..."
"My goodness!" the teacher exclaimed. "Is he alright?"
"He must be," said the boy. "He stopped shouting for help yesterday!"

Which skeleton wears a kilt?
Boney Prince Charlie!

Did you hear about the lazy skeleton?
He was bone idle!

What do you call a stupid skeleton?
Bonehead!

What happened to the skeleton who stayed by the fire too long?
He became bone dry!

Do you know the story about the body-snatchers?
Well, I won't tell you. You might get carried away!

Why do cemeteries have fences around them?
Because people are dying to get in!

Why did the skeleton pupil stay late at school?
He was boning up for his exams!

How do skeletons get their mail?
By bony express!

Who's a skeleton's favorite rock star?
Jon Bone Jovi!

Did you hear about the guy that lost his left arm and leg in a car crash?
He's all right now!

Three drunks were stumbling home late one night and found themselves by the old graveyard. "Come have a look over here," says one, "It's Michael Smith's grave, God bless his soul, he lived to the ripe old age of 87."
"That's nothing," says another, "here's one named Patrick Jones. It says here that he was 95 when he died."
Just then, the third yells out, "But here's a fella that died when he was 185!"
"What was his name?" asks the first drunk.
The third drunk lights a match to see what else is written on the stone, and says,
"Miles, from London."

Why did the skeleton go to hospital?
To have his ghoul stones removed!

LITTLE DEVILS!

Hee Hees from Hell

What is the best way to get rid of a demon?
Exorcise a lot!

What is the demons' favorite TV sit-com?
Fiends!

Why do demons and ghouls get on so well?
Because demons are a ghoul's best friend!

What happened to the demon who fell in the marmalade jar?
Nothing, he was a jammy devil!

What do demons have on holiday?
A devil of a time!

What's a devil's picket line called?
A demon-stration!

ATTACK OF THE MONSTERS!

A Feast of Beasts

Igor: Baron Frankenstein is funny, isn't he?
Monster: He puts me in stitches!

Why was Baron Frankenstein never lonely?
Because he was good at making new friends!

What was the inscription on the tomb of Frankenstein's monster?
MAY HE REST IN PIECES!

What do you call a clever monster?
Frank Einstein!

Where do you find monster snails?
On the end of monsters' fingers!

How did Frankenstein's monster eat his lunch?
He bolted it down!

A monster went to the doctor because he didn't feel well.
"What do you eat?" asked the doctor.
"For breakfast I have a couple of red snooker balls, and at lunchtime I grab a black, a pink and two yellows. I have a brown with my tea in the afternoon, and then a blue and another pink for dinner."
"I know why you are not feeling well," exclaimed the doctor. "You're not getting enough greens!"

Monster: Doctor, doctor, I need to lose 30 pounds of unsightly flab.
Doctor: Alright, I'll cut your head off.

What do you do with a green monster?
Ripen it on the window sill!

Why are monsters so forgetful?
Because everything you tell them goes in one ear and out the others!

Mommy monster: Don't eat that uranium.
Little monster: Why not?
Mommy monster: You'll get atomic-ache!

What happened to Ray when he met the man-eating monster?
He became an ex-Ray!

Monster: How much do you charge for dinner here?
Waiter: $20 a head, sir.
Monster: And how much for a couple of legs, as well?

What do you get if you cross a monster with a boy scout?
A monster that scares old ladies across the street!

GO

This little monster boy came home from school one day, crying his eyes out. "What's the matter darling?" asked his mother. "It's all the other children at school," he sobbed. "They keep teasing me and saying that I've got a big head." "You have not got a big head," said Mrs Monster, "Just ignore them. Now, will you do a little bit of shopping for me? I need a sack of potatoes, ten cartons of orange juice, a dozen loaves of bread, eight cabbages and a cauliflower." "Alright, Mom," said the little monster, "Where's your shopping bag?"

"Never mind about the bag," said Mrs Monster. "Just use your cap."

What's the difference between a monster and a mouse?

A monster makes bigger holes in the skirting board!

How do you make a monster fly?
Start with a ten-foot zip!

What do you get if you cross a monster with a watchdog?
Very nervous postmen!

How do you get a monster into a matchbox?
Take all the matches out first!

What time is it when a monster puts his left foot on your right foot?
Time to call an ambulance!

Why do some monsters have big ears?
Noddy wouldn't pay the ransom!

Mommy monster: Agatha, how often must I tell you not to eat with your fingers.
Agatha monster: Sorry, Mom.
Mommy monster: I should think so! Use a shovel like I do!

First monster: Am I late for dinner?
Second monster: Yes, everyone's been eaten.

What do you get if you cross a monster with a kangaroo?
Big holes all over Australia!

Little monster: Mom, I've finished. Can I leave the table?
Mommy monster: Yes, I'll save it for your tea.

A man was walking behind a hearse with a big monster on a lead. Behind them stretched a long line of mourners. "What happened?" asked a passer-by. "This monster bit my mother-in-law, and she died of fright." "Can I borrow it?" the passer-by asked.
The man pointed behind him: "Get in the queue," he said.

Monster: Where do fleas go in winter?
Werewolf: Search me!

There once was a monster called Fred,
Who used to eat garlic in bed;
His mother said, "Son,
That's not really done,
Why don't you eat people instead?"

What do you do with a blue monster?
Try and cheer him up!

How do you stop a monster from smelling?
Cut off his nose!

Did you hear about the girl monster who wasn't pretty and wasn't ugly?
She was pretty ugly!

Did you hear about the monster who ate a sofa and two chairs?
He had a suite tooth!

Did you hear about the two-headed monster at the freak show who went on strike for more money?
He said he had an extra mouth to feed!

What's big and hairy and goes "beep"?
A monster in a traffic jam.

How do monsters like their shepherd's pie?
With real shepherds!

How can you tell if a monster has a glass eye?
When it comes out in conversation!

How do monsters tell the future?
With horrorscopes!

How can you tell if there's a monster in your fridge?
You can't shut the door!

Monster lady: I have the face of a sixteen-year-old girl.
Monster boy: Well you'd better give it back. You're getting it all wrinkled!

What does a vegetarian monster eat?
Swedes!

What is big, slimy and ugly and blue?
A monster holding its breath!

Frankenstein's monster walks into a café and orders a cup of tea. "That'll be $3.95," said the waitress, when she brought it to him.
"You know, I was just thinking, we don't get many monsters in here ..."
"I'm not surprised, at these prices!" said the monster.

Why is the monsters' football field wet?
Because the players keep dribbling on it!

What did the monster want to eat in the restaurant?
The finger bowl!

What did the monster say when he ate a herd of gnus?
" ... and that's the end of the gnus!"

A very tall monster with several arms and legs, all of different lengths, went into a tailor's shop.
"I'd like to see a suit that will fit me," he told the tailor.
"So would I!" said the tailor.

If storks bring human babies, what brings monster babies?
Cranes!

Did you hear about the monster with five legs?
His trousers fit him like a glove!

Monster teacher: If I had two people beside me, and you had two people beside you, what would we have between us?
Monster pupil: Lunch!

Did you hear about the monster that has pedestrian eyes?
They look both ways before they cross!

What do you get if you cross a cyclops with peanut butter?
A monster that sticks to the roof of your mouth!

What's big and ugly and red all over?
An embarrassed monster!

Boy Monster: Is that your real face or are you wearing a gas-mask?
Girl Monster: I didn't come here to be insulted.
Boy: Oh, where do you usually go?

TOMB MUCH!

Fun with Mummies

What's a mummy's least favorite film?
Tomb Raider!

What's a mummy with a guitar and a drum?
A one-man bandage!

Why is it safe to tell a mummy your secret?
It'll keep it under wraps!

What kind of girl does a mummy take on a date?
Any old girl he can dig up!

Why were ancient Egyptian children confused?
Because their daddies were mummies!

Why was the mummy so tense?
He was all wound up!

Why couldn't the mummy come outside?
Because he was all wrapped up!

What is a mummy's favorite type of music?
Wrap!

How do you measure a mummy's house?
With a vault-meter!

Who's an impatient mummy driver?
Tooting car man!

Why don't mummies take vacations?
They're afraid they'll relax and unwind.

BLOOD GROUP!

Vampire Jokes

What happened in the vampires' race?
It finished neck and neck!

Why does Dracula have no friends?
Because he's a pain in the neck!

What happened to the two mad vampires?
They both went a little batty!

Where do vampires go on holiday?
To the Isle of Fright!

What do vampires send their heroes?
Fang-mail!

What is Dracula's favorite breakfast?
Readyneck!

Why are vampires hopeless at soccer?
Because they're afraid of crosses!

Why did the vampire give his girlfriend a blood test?
To see if she was his type!

How do vampires begin letters?
Tomb it may concern!

If a vampire was knocked out by Dracula in a fight what would he be?
Out for the count!

Where do Chinese vampires come from?
Fanghai!

What do vampires sing on New Year's Eve?
Auld Fang Syne!

What do vampires have for lunch?
Fangers and mash!

What is Dracula's favorite fruit?
Neck-tarines!

Why do vampires like school dinners?
Because they know they won't get stake!

What is a vampire's favorite soup?
Scream of tomato!

Did you hear about the vampire who died of a broken heart?
He had loved in vein!

Why was the young vampire a failure?
Because he fainted at the sight of blood!

What do you get when you cross a snowman with a vampire?
Frostbite!

Two nuns, Sister Marilyn and Sister Helen, are driving through Europe in their car. They get to Transylvania and stop at a traffic light. Suddenly, out of nowhere, Dracula jumps onto the front of the car and hisses through the windscreen. "Quick, quick!" shouts Sister Marilyn. "What shall we do?" "Show him your cross!" says Sister Helen. "Right!" says Sister Marilyn. She opens the window, shakes her fist and screams,

"Get off the car RIGHT NOW! I won't tell you again!!"

What do you get if you cross Dracula with Al Capone?

A fangster!

What's a vampire's favorite animal?

A giraffe, of course!

What do vampires like that are red and very silly?
Blood clots!

What do vampires make sandwiches out of?
Self-raising dead!

Why did the vampire take up acting?
It was in his blood!

What is Count Dracula's least favorite song?
"Vampires Burning, Vampires Burning"!

What do you get if you cross a vampire with a snail?
I don't know, but it would slow him down!

Why did the vampire enjoy ballroom dancing?
He could really get into the vaultz!

Why are vampire families so close?
Because blood is thicker than water!

What's Dracula's favorite coffee?
De-coffin-ated!

Dracula is thirsty one night and he sends a bat out to find him some fresh blood. The bat flies out of the window and comes back after three minutes, literally covered in blood from top to toe. Dracula is impressed. "Where did you get all that?" he asks. And the bat replies: "Do you see that tall church steeple over there on the horizon?" Dracula squints out of the window. "Yes, I see it!" he says.
And the bat says, "Well, I didn't."

What did the vampire call his electric toothbrush?
A newfangled device!

What happened when the vampire went to the blood bank?
He asked to make a withdrawal!

If you want to know more about Dracula, what do you have to do?
Join his fang club!

How do vampires keep their breath smelling nice?
They use extractor fangs!

Did you know that Dracula wants to become a comedian?
He's looking for a crypt-writer!

Which flavor ice cream is Dracula's favorite?
Vein-illa!

What is the first thing that vampires learn at school?
The alphabat!

Why is Hollywood full of vampires?
They need someone to play the bit parts!

What does a weight-conscious vampire drink?
Blood Light!

What's Dracula's favorite beer?
Bloodweiser!

What did the teacher say to Dracula after he failed his maths test?
Can't you count, Dracula?

How can you tell when a vampire has been in a bakery?
All the jam has gone from the doughnuts!

What is a vampire's favorite holiday?
Fangsgiving!

What did the kid vampire say to his mummy at bedtime?
"Mummy, turn off the switch.
I'm afraid of the light!"

What did Dracula say to his new apprentice?
We could do with some new blood around here!

Count Dracula was walking in the street at night when he was hit on the back of the head with a cocktail sausage. He looked around but there was nobody there. He walked on and was hit on the back of the head with a small pickled onion. He looked around ... nobody there ... he walked on again and was struck by a miniature Cornish pasty. He looked around, but could see nobody there. Eventually, he felt a tap on the shoulder. As he turned around, he was stabbed in the heart by a young woman holding a cocktail stick. As he lay dying, he hissed at the woman, "Who are you?"
She said: "I'm Buffet the Vampire Slayer!"

Where is Dracula's American office?
The Vampire State Building!

Where do vampires keep their savings?
In blood banks!

What does a vampire say to the mirror?
Terror, terror on the wall!

Why are vampires easy to tease?
Because they're suckers!

Was Dracula ever married?
No, he was a bat-chelor!

What did the vampire say after he had been to the dentist?
Fangs very much!

How does a vampire get through life with only one fang?
He has to grin and bare it!

A man's car broke down on a cold and wind-swept night, near an eerie-looking castle in Transylvania. The wizened old butler invited him to stay the night, and showed him to his room. It was dark and dirty, and the man was scared.
"I hope you'll be comfortable," said the butler.
"But if you need anything during the night, just scream ..."

What is red, sweet and bites people?
A jampire!

Why won't anyone kiss Dracula?
He has bat breath!

What kind of dog does Dracula have?
A bloodhound!

What's fast food to a vampire?
Someone with high blood pressure!

How does a girl vampire flirt?
She bats her eyes!

What do you get if you cross Dracula with Sir Lancelot?
A bite in shining armor!

Why do vampires hate arguments?
Because they make themselves cross!

Why are vampires like false teeth?
They all come out at night!

Bob: Why do you keep throwing bunches of garlic out of the window?
Terry: To keep the vampires away.
Bob: But there are no vampires around here.
Terry: See? It works!

Why does Dracula consider himself a good artist?
Because he likes to draw blood!

THE ICEMAN COMETH!

Yeti Spaghetti

What kind of money do yetis use?
Iced lolly!

What do you get if you cross a yeti with a kangaroo?
A fur coat with big pockets!

What do you get if you cross an elephant with the Abominable Snowman?
A jumbo yeti!

What do you call a yeti in a phone box?
Stuck!

What do yetis eat on top of Mount Everest?
High tea!

How does a yeti get to work?
By icicle!

What kind of man doesn't like to sit in front of the fire?
An Abominable Snowman!

What do Abominable Snowmen call their offspring?
Chill-dren!

Where do Abominable Snowmen go to dance?
To snowballs!

Why did the Abominable Snowman send his father to Siberia?
Because he wanted a frozen pop!

What did one Abominable Snowman say to the other?
I'm afraid I just don't believe in people!

How did the yeti feel when he had 'flu?
Abominable!

What is the Abominable Snowman's favorite book?
War and Frozen Peas!

Where are yetis found?
They're so big they're hardly ever lost!

When should you feed yeti's milk to a baby?
When it's a baby yeti!

Where do you find wild yetis?
It depends where you left them!

What does a yeti eat for dinner?
Ice-burgers!

Doctor, doctor, I keep thinking I'm the Abominable Snowman.
Keep cool!

FRIENDS FOR DINNER?

Cannibal Jokes

What did the cannibal do when he saw an "All you can eat" restaurant?
He had two waiters and a chef!

Why did the cannibal rush over to the cafeteria?
He heard children were half price!

Did you hear about the cannibal who was expelled from school?
He was buttering up his teacher!

What did the cannibal say when he came home and found his wife chopping up a python and a dwarf?
"Oh no. Not snake and pygmy pie again!"

What happened when the cannibal crossed the Atlantic on the QE2?
He told the waiter to take the menu away and bring him the passenger list!

What do cannibals eat at parties?
Buttered host!

What happened to the old cannibal who put in his false teeth back to front?
He ate himself!

A little cannibal came running into the house saying "Mom, Dad's fallen on the bonfire!"
Mom said, "Great, we'll have a barbecue!"

What is a cannibal's favorite food?
Baked beings!

How can you help a starving cannibal?
Give him a hand!

Why did the cannibal live on his own?
He was fed up with other people!

Why don't cannibals eat weathermen?
Because they give them wind!

What happened when the cannibals ate a comedian?
They had a feast of fun!

What did the cannibal mom say to her son who was chasing a missionary?
"Stop playing with your food!"

What do cannibal secretaries do with leftover fingernails?
They file them!

Reporter: Why are you living on a sugar plantation?
Scottish cannibal: So that I can feed my lads with molasses!

Why was the cannibal fined by the judge?
He was caught poaching!

What was the cannibal called who ate his father's sister?
An aunt-eater!

Why would the cannibal eat only babies?
He was on a diet!

What happens if you upset a cannibal?
You get into hot water!

What happened to the cannibal lion?
He had to swallow his pride!

What does a cannibal call a skateboarder?
Meals on wheels!

What did the cannibal's parents say when she brought her boyfriend home?
"Lovely, dear, he looks good enough to eat!"

RETURN OF THE MONSTERS!

More Monstrous Mayhem

What makes an ideal present for a monster?
Five pairs of gloves - one for each hand!

What's big, heavy, furry, dangerous and has 16 wheels?
A monster on roller-skates!

Why did the monster have green ears and a red nose?
So that he could hide in rhubarb patches!

What can a monster do that you can't do?
Count up to 25 on his fingers!

What do you give a monster with big feet?
Big shoes!

What do you get if you cross a plum with a man-eating monster?
A purple people-eater!

Why did the monster eat a light bulb?
Because he was in need of light refreshment!

What happens if a big, hairy monster sits in front of you at the cinema?
You miss most of the film!

Why was the monster top of the class at school?
Because two heads are better than one!

"Doctor, doctor, you must help me."
"What's the problem?"
"Every night, I dream there are terrible green and yellow slimy monsters under my bed. What on earth can I do?"
"Saw the legs off your bed."

Girl: Mom! A monster's just bitten my foot off!
Mom: Well, keep out of the kitchen, I've just washed the floor!

Did you hear about the monster who sent his picture to a lonely hearts club?
They sent it back saying they weren't that lonely!

Monster: When my grandfather was born, they passed out cigars. When my father was born, they passed out champagne.
When I was born, they just passed out!

How do you communicate with the Loch Ness Monster at 20,000 fathoms?
Drop him a line!

What do you get if a huge hairy monster steps on Batman and Robin?
Flatman and Ribbon!

First monster: What is that son of yours doing these days?
Second monster: He's at medical school.
First monster: Oh, what's he studying?
Second monster: Nothing, they're studying him!

A monster walked into the rent office with a $5 bill stuck in one ear and a $10 bill in the other.
You see, she was $15 in arrears!

Did you hear about the monster with one eye at the back of his head, and one at the front?
He couldn't see eye to eye with himself!

What is 20 yards long, ugly, and sings "Scotland the Brave"?
The Loch Ness Songster!

What did the Loch Ness Monster say to a beached whale?
Long time, no sea!

First monster: We had burglars last night.
Second monster: Oh, did you?
First monster: Well, it made a change from slime on toast ...

What do young female monsters do at parties?
They go around looking for edible bachelors!

Why are monsters big and hairy?
So that you can tell them apart from gooseberries ...

Cross-eyed monster: When I grow up I want to be a bus driver.
Witch: Well, I won't stand in your way!

How do you tell a good monster from a bad one?
If it's a good one, you'll be able to talk about it later!

What happened when two huge monsters ran in a race?
One ran in short bursts, the other ran in burst shorts!

What kind of monster can sit on the end of your finger?
The bogeyman!

How do you know when there's a monster under your bed?
Your nose touches the ceiling!

How can you tell the difference between a monster and a banana?
Try picking it up. If you can't, it's either a monster or a very heavy banana.

Did you hear about the monster who was known as Star Trek?
He had a left ear, a right ear and a final front ear!

What did they say about the aristocratic monster?
That he was born with a silver shovel in his mouth!

Why do monsters wear glasses?
So they don't bump into other monsters!

How do you greet a three-headed monster?
Hello, hello, hello!

How do you know that there's a monster in your bath?
You can't get the shower curtain closed!

What kind of monster has the best hearing?
The eeriest!

Mr Monster: Oi, hurry up with my supper!
Mrs Monster: Oh, do be quiet – I've only got three pairs of hands!

How do you address a 60-foot monster?
Very politely!

Why did the monster have to buy two tickets for the zoo?
One to get in and one to get out!

Why did the monster drink ten gallons of antifreeze?
So he didn't have to buy a coat!

What did one of the monster's eyes say to the other?
Between us is something that smells!

Did you hear about the monster who had eight arms?
He said they came in handy!

How do you keep an ugly monster in suspense?
I'll tell you tomorrow!

What happened when the monster fell down a well?
He kicked the bucket!

Bobby: The police are looking for a monster with one eye.
Johnny: Why don't they use two?

What time is it when a monster sits on your car?
Time to get a new car!

What do 20 monsters play when they are on the bus?
Squash!

What should you do if a monster runs through your front door?
Run through the back door!

What's big and ugly and wears sunglasses?
A monster on holiday!

MOON HOWLERS!

Werewolf Wit

How does a werewolf sign his letters?
Best vicious!

Why was the werewolf arrested in the butcher's shop?
He was chop-lifting!

How do you stop a werewolf howling in the back of a car?
Put him in the front!

Where does a werewolf sit in the cinema?
Anywhere he wants to!

What do you call a hairy beast that's lost?
A where-wolf!

What happened when the werewolf swallowed a clock?
He got ticks!

What happened when the werewolf chewed a bone for an hour?
When he got up, he only had three legs!

Mommy, Mommy, what's a werewolf?
Don't worry about that and comb your face!

Why did the boy take an aspirin after hearing a werewolf howl?
Because it gave him an eerie ache!

Why shouldn't you grab a werewolf by its tail?
It might be the werewolf's tail but it could be the end of you!

What do you call a hairy beast that no longer exists?
A were-wolf!

What do you get if you cross a witch with a werewolf?
A mad dog that chases airplanes!

Doctor: I'm sorry, madam, but I have to tell you that you are a werewolf.
Patient: Give me a piece of paper.
Doctor: Do you want to write your will?
Patient: No, a list of people I want to bite!

How do you know that a werewolf's been in the fridge?
There are paw prints in the butter!

How do you know that two werewolves have been in the fridge?
There are two sets of paw prints in the butter.

What do you call a werewolf with no legs?
Anything you like – he's not going to catch you!

What happens if you cross a werewolf with a sheep?
You have to get a new sheep!

What's fearsome, hairy and drinks from the wrong side of a glass?
A werewolf with hiccups!

How do you stop a werewolf attacking you?
Throw a stick and shout fetch!

What do you call a hairy beast in a river?
A weir-wolf!

What happened when the wolf fell in the washing machine?
He became a wash and werewolf!

Who are some of the werewolves' cousins?
The whatwolves and whenwolves!

HAGS OF FUN!

Witches and Wizards

What do you call a motor bike belonging to a witch?
A broooooooom stick!

What has a black hat, flies on a broomstick, and can't see anything?
A witch with her eyes shut!

Why did the witch stand up in front of the audience?
She had to give a screech!

What did the doctor say to the witch in hospital?
With any luck you'll soon be well enough to get up for a spell!

What does a witch enjoy cooking most?
Gnomelettes!

When can you tell when witches are carrying a time-bomb?
You can hear their brooms tick!

What is old, ugly and blue?
A witch holding her breath!

What do witches sing at Christmas?
"Deck the halls with poison ivy ...."

How do you know when you are in bed with a witch?
She has a big "W" embroidered on her pyjamas!

What did one witch say to another when they left the cinema?
Do you want to walk home or shall we take the broom?

BROOM
STOP

How do you picture yourself flying on a broom?
Witchful thinking!

What is a witch with poison ivy called?
An itchy witchy!

What do witches put on their hair?
Scare spray!

What was the witches' favorite subject in school?
Spelling!

Who was the most famous witch detective?
Warlock Holmes!

What is the difference between a witch and the letters M A K E S?
One makes spells and the other spells makes!

Why don't witches like to ride their brooms when they're angry?
They don't want to fly off the handle!

Have you heard about the good weather witch?
She's forecasting sunny spells!

How do witches tell the time?
By looking at their witch watches!

What happens if you see twin witches?
You won't be able to see which witch is witch!

What has six legs and flies?
A witch giving her cat a ride!

What sits in a tree with her thumb out?
A witch-hiker!

What has handles and flies?
A witch in a dustbin!

Why did the witch put her broom in the wash?
She wanted a clean sweep!

Why did the witch give up fortune-telling?
There was no future in it!

How did the witch almost lose her baby?
She didn't take it far enough into the woods!

What do witches race on?
Vroomsticks!

How do witches lose weight?
They join weight witches!

What goes cackle, cackle, bonk?
A witch laughing her head off!

Why do witches have stiff joints?
They get broomatism!

Why do witches wear pointy black hats?
To keep their heads warm!

What did the wizard say to his witch girlfriend?
Hello gore-juice!

What does a witch get if she is a poor traveller?
Broom sick!

Where do witches keep their purses?
In hag bags!

What is the difference between a deer running away and a small witch?
One's a hunted stag and the other is a stunted hag!

What happened to the naughty little witch at school?
She was ex-spelled!

How is the witches' team doing?
They're having a spell in the second division!

What's evil and goes up and down?
A witch in a lift!

Why do cats prefer wizards to witches?
Because the sorcerers often have milk in them!

Why did the witch feed her cat with pennies?
She wanted to put some money in the kitty!

What do you call a witch made of cotton who has lots of holes in her?
A string hag!

Why do witches ride on broomsticks?
Because it's quicker than walking!

What do you get if you cross a dinosaur with a wizard?
A Tyrannosaurus hex!

What name did the witch give to her cooking pot?
It's called-Ron!

Why didn't the witch sing at the concert?
Because she had a frog in her throat!

What do you call a witch who drives badly?
A road hag!

How do you get milk from a witches' cat?
Steal her saucer!

Why do black cats never shave?
Because 8 out of 10 cats prefer whiskas!

What do witches' cats like for breakfast?
Mice krispies!

What do you call a witch who murders her mom and dad?
An orphan!

What do you get if you cross a sorceress with a millionaire?
A very witch person!

What do little witches do after school?
Their gnomework!

What sound does a witch make when she cries?
"Brew-hoo, Brew-hoo"!

How do you make a witch float?
Two scoops of ice cream, a glass of coke and a witch!

What happens when a flying witch breaks the sound barrier?
You hear the sonic broom!

What do you get if you cross a witch and an iceberg?
A cold spell!

DEAD MEN WALKING!

Zombie and Son

What did the zombie do when his hand fell off?
He went to the secondhand shop!

Who do zombie cowboys fight?
Deadskins!

How do you know a zombie is tired?
He's dead on his feet!

What did the zombie's friend say when he introduced him to his girlfriend?
"Good grief! Where did you dig her up from?"

Why did the zombie crash his car?
He left his foot on the accelerator!

What do baby zombies play with?
Deady bears!

Where do zombies go for cruises?
The Deaditerranean!

What did the zombie get his medal for?
Deadication!

What do little zombies play?
Corpses and Robbers!

Doctor: Are you still having trouble with your breathing?
Zombie: Yes, I am.
Doctor: We'll see if we can put a stop to that!

What did one zombie say to another?
"Get a life!"

A zombie tripped over his headstone one day and broke it.
"Oh no!" he said, "That's gonna cost me an arm and a leg!"

Did you hear about the zombie card game?
One guy threw his hand in, one guy cried his eyes out, and the other one laughed his head off!

What's cuter than a zombie baby?
A zombie baby with a bunny in its mouth!

What did the Zombie mummy say to the Zombie baby?
"You have your father's eyes. Give them back!"

What's blue, covered with frost, and sits next to a turkey?
A zombie in the freezer!

What's black and white and red all over?
A nun being eaten by zombies!

How can you tell if a Valentine's card is from a zombie?
The tongue's still in the envelope!

WAIT! THEY'RE STILL ALIVE!

Yet More Monsters

What do you get if you cross a fashion designer with a sea monster?
The Loch Dress Monster!

What is large, yellow, lives in Scotland and has never been seen?
The Loch Ness Canary!

Boy: Mom, why can't I swim in Loch Ness?
Mother: Because there are monsters in it.
Boy: But Dad's swimming there.
Mother: That's different. He's insured.

What do you get if you cross the Loch Ness Monster with a shark?
Loch Jaws!

How do you get to the monster's house?
Walk down the street, then turn fright at the dead end!

What's a monster's favorite play?
Romeo and Ghouliet!

What's a monster's favorite vegetable?
A human bean!

What do you get if you cross a monster with a teacup?
An ugly mug!

What position does a monster play on the soccer team?
Ghoulie!

Why did the monster knit herself three socks?
Because she grew another foot!

Where is the monster's temple?
On the side of his head!

What trees do monsters like best?
Ceme-trees!

What happens when monsters hold beauty contests?
Nobody wins!

What do you get if you cross a monster with a pig?
Huge chops!

What's the difference between monsters and magnets?
Monsters are unattractive!

First monster: That girl over there just rolled her eyes at me.
Second monster: Well, roll them back, she might need them.

What did the grandfather monster say to his grandson when they hadn't seen each other for quite a while?
You gruesome!

What do you get if you cross a monster with a pigeon?
Lots of very worried pedestrians!

Knock knock.
Who's there?
Turner.
Turner who?
Turner round, there's a monster breathing down your neck!

On which day do monsters eat people?
Chewsday!

What's ugly and easy to hold?
A monster on a stick!

A man who never went to church was spending a quiet day fishing, when suddenly his boat was attacked by the Loch Ness Monster. In one easy flip, the beast tossed him and his boat high into the air then opened its mouth to swallow both. As the man sailed head over heels, he cried out, "Oh my God! Help me!"

At once, the ferocious attack scene froze in place and, as the man hung in mid-air, a booming voice came down from the clouds.

"I thought you didn't believe in Me!"

"Come on, God, give me a break!" the man pleaded. "Two minutes ago I didn't believe in the Loch Ness Monster either!"

Why are monsters covered in wrinkles?
Have you ever tried to iron a monster?

What do you get if you cross a monster with a skunk?
A big, ugly smell!

Where do monsters go in the summer?
On their horrid-days!

What type of monster really loves dance music?
The boogieman!

What is big, red and prickly, has three eyes and eats rocks?
A big, red, prickly three-eyed rock-eater!

Did you hear about the monster who had an extra pair of hands? Where did she keep them?
In her handbag!

Little monster: I can't do my homework – my head aches!
Mommy monster: Don't be silly – use the other one!

What do you call a monster with a wooden head?
Edward
What do you call a monster with two wooden heads?
Edward Woodward.
What do you call a monster with four wooden heads?
I don't know but Edward Woodward would!

Did you hear about the monster who went on a crash diet?
He wrecked three cars and a bus!

Did you hear about the monster who had twelve arms and no legs?
He was all fingers and thumbs!

Did you hear about the two-headed monster at the freak show who went on strike for more money?
He claimed he had an extra mouth to feed!

MONKEY BUSINESS!

King Kong Crackers

What is as big as King Kong but doesn't weigh anything?
King Kong's shadow!

What do you get if you cross King Kong with a watchdog?
A terrified postman!

Why did King Kong paint the bottoms of his feet brown?
So that he could hide upside down in a jar of peanut butter!

What happened when King Kong swallowed Big Ben?
He found it time-consuming!

What do you get if you cross King Kong with a parrot?
A very messy cage!

Two policemen in New York were watching King Kong climb up the Empire State Building. One said to the other, "What do you think he's doing?" "It's obvious," replied his colleague,
"he wants to catch a plane!"

What might you find between King Kong's toes?
Slow-running natives!

What is a giant monkey's table tennis tune called?
"King Kong's ping pong sing song"!

How do you catch King Kong?
Hang upside down and make a noise like a banana!

What do you get if you cross King Kong with a frog?
A gorilla that catches airplanes with its tongue!

What would you get if you crossed King Kong with a skunk?
I don't know, but it could always get a seat on a bus!

Where does King Kong sleep?
Anywhere he wants to!

What should you do if you are on a picnic with King Kong?
Give him the biggest bananas!

What do you get if King Kong sits on your best friend?
A flat mate!

How can you mend King Kong?
With a monkey wrench!

BOO TO YOU TOO!

Ghostly Gags

When do ghosts usually appear?
Just before someone screams!

What should you say when you meet a ghost?
How do you boo!

What do ghosts eat for breakfast?
Dreaded wheat!

What do ghosts eat for lunch?
Ghoul-ash!

What did the papa ghost say to the baby ghost?
Fasten your sheet belt!

Who is the most important member of the ghost's football team?
The ghoulie!

How do ghosts like their eggs cooked?
Terrifried!

How do you know if you're being haunted by a parrot?
He keeps going: "Whoooo's a pretty boy then?"

Where do ghost trains stop?
At devil crossings!

What airline do ghouls fly with?
British Scareways!

What do ghosts eat for supper?
Spook-etti!

What do you call a drunken ghost?
A methylated spirit!

What do Chinese ghouls like to eat?
Terrifried rice!

What's a ghost's favorite fruit?
Booberries!

What do you call a ghost with a broken leg?
Hoblin goblin!

Why did the ghost cross the road?
To get to "The Other Side"!

Who does a ghost fall in love with?
His ghoul friend!

What tops off a ghost's apple pie?
Whipped scream!

What happened when the ghost asked for a whisky at his local bar?
The bartender said: "Sorry sir, we don't serve spirits here!"

Why did the ghost go into the bar?
For the boos!

Why did the game warden arrest the ghost?
He didn't have a haunting license!

Jeff: My sister wanted to marry a ghost.
Bob: Good grief. Why?
Jeff: I don't know what possessed her!

What do you call a ghost's mother and father?
Transparents!

Why did the ghost go to the funfair?
He wanted to go on a rollerghoster!

What do young ghouls write their homework in?
Exorcise books!

What happens when a ghost haunts a theatre?
The actors get stage fright!

What do you call a spirit who gets too close to the fire?
Toasty ghosty!

What happens when a ghost gets lost in a fog?
He's mist!

Where do ghosts go to work?
At the ghost office!

What does a hungry ghost want?
Ice-cream!

What do you get when you cross Bambi with a ghost?
Bamboo!

What kind of mistakes do spooks make?
Boo boos!

What do ghosts dance to?
Soul music!

TERRIBLE TITTERS!

Assorted Horrible Humour

A very posh man was walking around an art gallery, when he stopped by one particular exhibit.
"I suppose this picture of a hideous monster is what you call modern art?" he said very pompously.
"No, sir," replied the assistant, "that's what we call a mirror."

When is a bogey-man most likely to enter your bedroom?
When the door is open!

What did Godzilla say when he saw the 7.30 to Waterloo Station?
Oh good! A chew chew train!

"Doctor, doctor, you've got to help me – I keep dreaming of bats, creepy-crawlies, demons, ghosts, monsters, vampires, werewolves and yetis!"
"How very interesting! Do you always dream in alphabetical order?"

Why were there screams coming from the kitchen?
The cook was beating the eggs and whipping the cream!

What eats its victims two by two?
Noah's shark!

What weighed 300 pounds and terrorized Paris?
The Fat-Tum of the Opera!

Waiter, waiter! There's a slug in my salad.
I'm sorry, sir, I didn't know you were a vegetarian!

What's green, seven feet tall, and mopes in the corner?
The Incredible Sulk!

What's green and wrinkly?
The Incredible Hulk's gran!

Johnny: Dad, what has a purple body with yellow spots, eight hairy legs and big slimy eyes on stalks?
Dad: I don't know. Why?
Johnny: Because one's just crawled up your trouser leg!

How do you talk to a giant?
Use big words!

When do banshees howl?
Moanday night!

What does a headless horseman ride?
A nightmare!

What do you call serious rocks?
Gravestones!

Have you seen Quasimodo?
I have a hunch he's back!

How did the headless horseman do in the Derby?
He won by a neck!

What do stupid kids do at Halloween?
They carve a face on an apple and go bobbing for pumpkins!

How do you get the most apples when bobbing at Halloween?
Wear a snorkel!

What's a goblin's favorite flavor?
Lemon 'n' Slime!

Ten books at bedtime ...

On the Trail of the Body Snatchers
by Hugh Duneit

Mysterious Murders
by Ivor Cloo

Keeping Snakes
by Sir Pent

Vampires at Large
by B. Warned

Chased by a Werewolf
by Claude Bottom

The Bad-tempered Werewolf
by Claudia Armoff

The Vampire's Victim
by E. Drew-Bludd

Never Make a Witch Angry
by Sheila Tack

Ghost Stories
by I.M. Scared

Going on a Witch Hunt
by Count Miout

What happened when the canary flew into Bigfoot?
Shredded tweet!

What is green and tough?
A toad with a machine gun.

What did Roman giants wear?
Ogre togas!

What do you call a snake that informs the police?
A grass snake!

What's magic, wears glasses and goes "ring ring"?
Harry Potter and the philosopher's phone!

Boy: Dad! Come out! Mom's fighting this ten-foot gargoyle with three heads!
Dad: I'm not coming out – he'll have to look after himself.

PART 2
MONSTER FACTS

THE VAMPIRE STRIKES BACK

The Real Count Dracula

The rugged Transylvanian Alps provide one of the most spectacular landscapes in Europe. Hawks soar around the snow-covered mountain peaks and bears stalk the forests below. Medieval villages and the ruins of mighty castles can abruptly appear through the fog.

Transylvania also produced a leader known as a defender of the Christian faith, a Romanian hero, and a subhuman monster. His name was Prince Vlad, but the world knows him by another name: Dracula.

Vlad was born in 1431 into a noble family. His father was called "Dracul," meaning

"dragon" or "devil" in Romanian, because he belonged to the Order of the Dragon, a Christian group at war with the Muslim Ottoman Empire. "Dracula" means "son of Dracul"', but also "son of the devil". Scholars believe this nickname was probably the source of the legend of Dracula.

He grew up in an unstable and dangerous world, his country constantly at war. Dracula's father was murdered, while his older brother, Mircea, was blinded with red-hot iron stakes and buried alive by his enemies.

From 1448 until his death in 1476, Dracula ruled Walachia and Transylvania, both part of Romania today. The church praised him for defending Christianity, but disapproved of his cruel methods, which became infamous.

Dracula earned another nickname, "Vlad Tepes", which means "Vlad the Impaler". Dracula's favorite method of torture was to throw people onto wooden stakes and leave them to writhe in agony, often for days. As a warning to others, the bodies would remain on the stakes as vultures and crows ate the rotting flesh.

During one battle with the Turks, Dracula retreated into nearby mountains, impaling captured people as he went. The Turkish advance was halted because the sultan could not bear the stench from the decaying corpses.

The British newspaper *The Daily Telegraph* reported on Halloween 2000 that Ottomar Rudolphe Vlad Dracula Prince Kretzulesco was looking for a medieval castle in England where he could live and work. Born Otto Berbig, the Prince was adopted by the late Princess Katharina Olympia Caradja, a direct descendant of Dracula himself.

FOR SALE
ESTATE AGENT

Dracula was reported to have eaten a meal on a table set up amidst hundreds of impaled victims. He was also reported to have occasionally eaten bread dipped in a victim's blood.

Nicholas of Modrussa, Papal envoy in Buda (now Budapest), Hungary, wrote to Pope Pius II that Dracula had massacred 40,000 men, women and children of all ages and nationalities in one incident in 1464. Gabriele Rangone, bishop of Erlau, stated in 1475 that Dracula had personally ordered the murders of 100,000 people, or close to one-fifth of the population under his rule.

Dracula was killed in December 1476 fighting the Turks near Bucharest, Romania. His head was cut off and displayed in the city of Constantinople. He was buried at the Snagov Monastery

near Bucharest. The monastery was also used as a prison and torture chamber, where unsuspecting prisoners praying before an icon of the Virgin Mary would fall through a trapdoor onto sharp stakes below.

In 1931 archaeologists searching Snagov found a coffin covered in a purple shroud embroidered with gold. The skeleton inside was covered with silk brocade, matching a shirt depicted in an old painting of Dracula. A ring, matching those worn by the Order of the Dragon, was sewn into a shirtsleeve.

The contents of the coffin were taken to the History Museum in Bucharest but have since disappeared without a trace, leaving the mysteries of the real Prince Dracula unanswered.

Romania's former Communist dictator, Nicolae Ceauşescu, admired Dracula and portrayed him as a national hero, downplaying his atrocities. The 500th anniversary of Dracula's death was observed in 1976 with various celebrations, including a commemorative postage stamp. In 1989, when the Ceaușescu regime was toppled and mobs in Bucharest attempted to storm the government, the dictator and his wife fled to their palace near Snagov, where Dracula was buried. The Ceaușescus were captured and shot by a firing squad near Dracula's castle.

Belief in vampires and the power of blood is as old as mankind. Early man smeared himself in blood and sometimes drank it. The ancient Chinese, Egyptians, Babylonians, Greeks, and Romans all believed in vampires. The Jewish Talmud tells of Lilith, Adam's disobedient first wife, who was transformed into a monster roaming the night.

Some doctors believe that old peasant tales of aristocratic "vampires" living in nearby castles could be based on medical fact. Some of the traits attributed to vampires – sensitivity to light, fangs, pale skin – may describe the symptoms of certain illnesses. For example, the hereditary blood disease porphyria was believed to be rife among the Eastern European aristocracy. People with porphyria become extremely sensitive to light, develop skin lesions, and get brown or reddish teeth. Physicians at the time sometimes told patients to drink blood from other people to build up their strength.

Rabies, which is spread by animals such as wolves or bats (both associated with vampires), may also have been endemic in Transylvania in Dracula's day. Rabies symptoms include insomnia, madness and hallucinations. Modern treatment for rabies includes immune globulin, a protein found in blood.

In Transylvania, with its blend of Hungarian, Romanian and gypsy folklore, belief in vampires has always been strong. Orthodox Christians believe the soul does not leave the body for the afterlife until 40 days after burial. When an Orthodox Christian is thrown out of the Church, or converts to another faith, it is said that the earth will no longer receive his body, forcing him to wander the Earth undead.

In the Americas, the early Indians of Peru believed in devil worshippers who sucked the life-blood from sleeping youths, while the Aztecs sacrificed victims to ensure the Sun would continue to rise, removing the still-beating hearts from their victims and offering them up to the gods as a gift.

Vampire bats have fewer teeth than other bats because they don't have to chew their food.

LEAPING LIZARDS!

The Komodo Dragon

Komodo Dragons are no myth. They are huge, brown-grey lizards with powerful jaws, razor-sharp claws, and long tails. They have rounded snouts and curved, serrated teeth like a shark's. Movable joints and plates in their skulls enable them to shift their jaws so they can swallow large prey. Komodo Dragons can locate prey from several miles away by smelling it out with sensors on their long, forked tongues. The record size for a Komodo Dragon is more than ten feet in length and 365 pounds in weight.

There are over 3,000 lizard species in the world, and the Komodo Dragon, or

Varanus komodoensis, is the biggest. Its ancestors date back more than 100 million years. They live only on four remote Indonesian islands: Flores, Gili Motang, Komodo and Rinca, and are listed as a vulnerable species by the World Conservation Union. Around 5,000 of these animals exist today.

Komodo Dragons eat carrion (dead animal flesh) but also prey on deer, wild pigs, snakes, monkeys, livestock including goats and even buffalo and wild horses. Scientists believe that millions of years ago, Komodo Dragons hunted now-extinct Pygmy Elephants. Young Dragons feed on rodents, insects, lizards, birds, and their eggs.

An adult Dragon will hide along a trail and wait for an unsuspecting creature to walk by. Then, with long claws and short, sharp teeth, the Dragon attacks. If the prey escapes, the Dragon will simply follow it at a leisurely pace. That's because saliva in the Dragon's

bite contains a deadly bacteria that will eventually poison its intended meal. Once caught, prey is pinned down with a mighty claw and ripped to pieces by the Dragon's awesome jaws and teeth. After eating something big like a deer, a Dragon will sleep it off for up to a week.

Komodo Dragons have mouths full of flat, serrated teeth, highly adapted for cutting flesh. The teeth break off easily and are replaced frequently: a Dragon may grow as many as 200 new teeth each year.

Komodo Island is a national park set aside for the Dragons' protection. The Dragons used to be allowed to attack goats as a tourist attraction, but this activity was stopped in 1993 because it reduced the lizards' fear of humans, increasing the chances of a Dragon turning man-eater and eating the tourists for breakfast – something which has happened once or twice already.

Life for a young Komodo Dragon is no picnic. As soon as the baby hatches, it scrambles out of the nest and scurries up the nearest tree so it won't be eaten by its own mom and dad. Fortunately for the babies, the adults are too heavy to climb trees. The baby Dragons live in the branches eating eggs, grasshoppers and beetles until they are about four years old and three feet or so long, when they are big enough to look after themselves on the ground.

The Western world did not learn about these Dragons until 1912, when a pilot crash-landed near one of the islands. Since then, human settlements have put pressure on their habitat, but the population has remained stable, and the mighty lizards have become a lucrative tourist attraction, boosting the island economy.

IF YOU GO DOWN TO THE WOODS TODAY

Bigfoot: Half Man, Half Ape

In many remote areas of the world there have been sightings of a hair-covered, man-like creature. It is known by many names, and often claimed as being the "missing link" in evolution between the ape and the primitive human being. In the northwestern USA, this beast is known as "Bigfoot".

There are numerous sightings every year, even today. The descriptions of the creatures are very similar from sighting to sighting. Witnesses have reported the creatures to be anything from five feet to more than eight feet tall.

Bigfoot is far from being confined to North America. He is found in almost all parts of the world, and known by many names.

One of the most famous American Bigfoot sightings took place in the mid 1850s. Two trappers were camping in the woods. Returning to their camp one day, they found it ransacked, and massive footprints on the ground. The men, a little shaken, repaired their camp and got ready for supper.

The only rational – if a little unlikely – explanation the hunters could come up with for the footprints was that they were made by a huge bear walking on its hind legs. They concluded that no human could possibly have made them. One of the men was awakened that night by the sounds of an

intruder. He saw a large figure at the entrance of their home-made shelter, and he could smell a foul smell. He grabbed his rifle and fired. The thing ran back to the woods. The trappers stayed awake for the rest of the night but there were no further visitations.

They continued setting out their traps the next day, staying close together for safety. When they returned to camp, it had been ransacked again. More two-legged footprints were found.

The men made a large fire and took turns guarding camp. Well into the night, the thing came back. They could hear it as it walked around the woods near the camp, making strange growling noises but it never came near their fire.

The next day the trappers decided, not surprisingly, to move on. All morning they stayed together, collecting up their traps from the day before. Both had the feeling of being watched, and they could hear twigs snapping in the woods nearby. Around noon, one left the other to return and pack up their camp.

When the second hunter returned with the traps in the late afternoon, a horrifying sight greeted him. His friend lay dead, his neck broken and four fang marks in his throat. More footprints were at the scene. That was it. The remaining trapper left everything behind. He didn't stop running until he got back to civilization.

In some parts of the US, the apeman is called Sasquatch. In various parts of Europe, he is known as Kaptar, Biabin-guli, Grendel, Ferla Mohir or Brenin Ilwyd. In Africa: Ngoloko or Kikomba. In Asia: Gin-sung, Mirygdy, Mecheny, Nguoi Rung or Yeti, and in Australia, the Yowie.

IT'S A DOG'S LIFE

The Facts about Werewolves

It is believed that humans and wolves evolved at around the same time: approximately 10,000 years BC.

In Greek myth, Lycaos was the extraordinarily cruel king of Arcadia. Lycaos sought favor with the great god Zeus by offering him the flesh of a young child. Enraged, Zeus turned Lycaos into a wolf. Over the centuries, the belief that certain people can turn themselves into animals – especially wolves – and roam the earth doing evil, became widespread.

In 400 BC, Damarchus, a supposed werewolf from Arcadia, was reported to have won boxing medals at the Olympic Games.

In the Middle Ages, many Europeans believed wolves were tools of the devil, and the animals were ruthlessly hunted. Epileptics and the mentally ill were often brought to court and accused of being werewolves. Between 1520 and 1630 there were over 30,000 werewolf trials in France alone.

In the year AD 930 Pope Leon was informed of two sorceresses in Germany who could transform others into animals. One of their victims was able to regain his human form by eating roses.

Today, psychologists use the term "lycanthrope" to describe a mentally ill person who actually believes he has been changed into an animal.

Werewolves supposedly love to eat babies and corpses.

The word "werewolf" means "manwolf" since "wer" is the Saxon word for man.

In mythology, silver bullets or arrows can kill a werewolf, but it is not guaranteed.

After death, a werewolf is said to resume his human identity.

It is believed that a werewolf waking as a human will still bear any wounds he or she acquired while in the werewolf state.

When someone changes into a werewolf, they are supposed to lose all control over their human mind and develop all the senses and thoughts of a wolf.

When a werewolf changes back into a human, he is supposed to have no recollection of the previous night's events.

The first werewolf movie was called *The Werewolf of London* and was released in 1935.

In Italy, the belief is that anybody born under a full moon on a Friday is likely to become a werewolf.

Werewolf hunters believe that you can get away from a werewolf and be safe by climbing up an ash tree.

Other popular beliefs are that werewolves turn into vampires after death, or that they are immortal. Vampire experts disagree!

The Middle Ages saw a peak in werewolf reports. In France between 1520 and 1630, over 30,000 *loup-garou* (werewolf) trials took place.

THEY STALK THE EARTH!

Actual Sightings of Freaky Creatures!

The Abominable Snowman

Known as "Metch-Kangmi" in Tibet, this is a huge, hairy creature that walks the Himalayas. For decades, explorers have reported huge footprints in the snow. An expedition on Mount Annapurna in 1970 spotted a large, furry creature walking on two legs on a nearby mountain. Climbers watched through binoculars for half an hour before it vanished in a clump of trees. Scientists believe bears could have left some of the footprints. However, the Sherpa people of the region have traditionally believed that the Himalayas are haunted by demons and spirits, while the Yeti, an ancient beast, prowls the mountains.

Amali

From the 1870s onwards, an English explorer named Alfred Smith spent a good deal of time in central Africa. In a memoir entitled, *TraderHorn*, he mentioned two animals, described by local villagers, that met no description of anything he'd ever heard of. He wrote: "The 'Jago-Nini' they say is still in the swamps and rivers, and I've seen the 'Amali's' footprints, they are about the size of a frying pan in circumference and with three claws instead of five." In the 1970s, American herpetologist (reptile expert) James Powell was conducting field research in Gabon, Africa. When he showed pictures of various animals to native informants, they most often compared the Amali to the Diplodocus, a long-necked sauropod dinosaur.

The Beast of Bodmin

This cat-like creature was thought responsible for the death of over 200 farm animals over a five-month period in England in 1987. The creature, and others like it, have been sighted numerous times since then and one was once clocked running at over 35 mph. The beast has also been seen to leap over six-foot-high fences without any difficulty. The most plausible explanation for the Beast is that it is an escaped big cat that is surviving in the wild.

Bunyip

Beginning in the 19th century, all the way through to 1932, an odd creature was often reported to have been seen in Australia. The "Bunyip" was semi-aquatic, bigger than a dog, with long, black hair and no tail. It had a horse-like head and long ears, but was never captured or identified. Today, the word "bunyip" refers to any imaginary, spooky animal that inspires laughter or fear.

Champ

In July 1883, Sheriff Nathan H. Mooney looked out on Lake Champlain in New York state, USA, and saw a gigantic water serpent about 50 yards away. It rose out of the water, was seven or eight yards long and close enough for the witness to see clearly some round white spots inside its mouth. Lake Champlain's monster is nicknamed "Champ", and has been sighted over 240 times. Champlain is a deep, freshwater lake, created some 10,000 years ago, and supports more than enough fish to feed a small group of lake monsters. The most significant photograph was taken on July 5, 1977 by Sandra Mansi of Connecticut. Mansi took a photo of what she thought was a "dinosaur" whose neck and head were some two yards out of the water. The Mansi photograph had been examined by scientists, who concluded that it has not been retouched or tampered with.

Chupacabras

This deadly killer rears its ugly head periodically in Latin America. Recently, the corpses of 800 animals – sheep, pigs, chicken, and dogs – have been found, drained of blood, in northern Chile. The bodies are invariably covered with strange bite-marks.The monster is described as a winged monkey, about eight feet tall, with long, clawed arms and hideous fangs.

Other eyewitnesses state that the creature resembles a flying rodent or a species of kangaroo.

In 1995, in Puerto Rico, Chupacabras allegedly killed eight sheep at once, leaving behind a pile of bloodless corpses. The beast has also struck in Texas, Costa Rica, and Mexico. Chupacabras could be a cousin of the vampire bat, three species of which live in parts of Mexico, Central and South America.

Duck-billed Platypus

When word of this creature first reached Europe in 1797, everyone thought it was an elaborate hoax. Even when stuffed specimens arrived, people suspected that parts of different animals were all glued together, and when they heard that it was an egg-laying mammal, they laughed even louder. Only when eminent scientists performed on-site observations of the animal in its natural habitat did the rest of the scientific world finally agree it really existed.

Kapre

Persistent reports from the islands of Luzon and Samarlead lead one to believe that Bigfoot has a cousin in the Philippines. Witnesses claim that the Kapre stands more than eight feet tall and is covered with hair. They say its face, hands, and feet are human-like, and it eats fruits, crabs, fish, and the occasional rat.

Loch Ness Monster

In 1933, a man and a woman claimed to have seen a lizard-like creature 12 to 15 yards long holding an animal in its jaws cross over a road and disappear into Loch Ness, Scotland. Nessie is more usually described as a giant creature with a huge, rounded body around 30 yards long, and a long neck. Some think it is a prehistoric sea-going dinosaur, possibly a pleiosaur. An expedition in 1934 at the height of "monster fever" claimed 21 sightings and took five pictures.

Scientists have speculated that Nessie is a large ocean fish, or eel, that has became stranded in the loch. However, Loch Ness is more than 200 yards deep. Little sunlight penetrates its depths, making photosynthesis difficult, so few plants or fish survive there. Although it is 22 miles long (the largest freshwater lake in Great Britain) and a monster could easily lurk undetected in the murky depths, the animal would not find much to eat. Since the larger public first became aware of it, the Loch Ness Monster has become an international media star, appearing in numerous movies, and even turning up on a commemorative stamp issued by the Maldive Islands.

De Loys' Ape

This creature was killed on the Venezuela/Columbia border in 1917 by one Francois De Loys and his party. It appears to be a very man-like ape, but has never been identified as a known species. The size and shape of the beast's forehead are unlike that of any of the known primates of South America. Theories as to its identity have suggested that it is a South American version of Bigfoot, or even the missing evolutionary link between human beings and apes.

Frogman of Loveland

This amphibian freak has been seen by numerous people around Loveland, Ohio, USA. Witnesses include police officers who have seen the creatures at the side of the road. Descriptions of the creature all seem to match. It is three to five feet tall, walks upright like a human, has webbed hands and feet, the head of a large frog and leathery skin.

Giant Congo Snake

In 1959 a photograph was taken by a Belgian helicopter pilot, Remy Van Lierde, while on patrol over the Congo. The snake he snapped measured 12 to 15 yards in length, and was brown and green with a white belly. It had triangular jaws and a yard-long head. Experts have verified the pictures as authentic. As the helicopter flew in lower, the snake raised its head up and made as if to strike at the helicopter.

Mapinguary

Hunters in South America's rainforest call it the "beast with the breath of hell". Residents of Brazil's Matto Grosso know it as the "Mapinguary". It is a giant two-legged beast that emits a stench so foul, that those who encounter it are rendered helpless. Zoologists who have studied the reports take them seriously. Some believe the creature to be a hitherto unknown type of ape.

Mawnan Owlman

In the 1970s, a silvery, feathered birdman was observed by people in Mawnan in Cornwall. The birdman was said to have pincers as feet, reddish eyes and a large mouth. Two sisters watched it fly over a church in 1976. In July of that same year there were more sightings of the creature, both on the ground and in the sky. From June to August of 1978 there were additional sightings in the area.

Mermaid

Henry Hudson was a famous English explorer of the 16th century – New York's Hudson River is named after him. He wrote in his journal on June 15, 1610: "This evening one of our company, looking overboard, saw a mermaid, and called up some of the company to see her, one more of the crew came up, and by that time she was close to the ship's side, looking earnestly on the men. A little after a wave came and overturned her."

Mid-east Thunderbird

In 1977, one of two large black birds with eight-foot wingspans tried to carry off ten-year-old Marlan Lowe in its claws one evening in Illinois, USA. Although experts say that no bird native to Illinois could possibly lift 65-pound Marlan, this is only one of many such encounters with huge black birds in the American Mid-east. They are described as Condor-like in appearance, with white stripes on the neck and massive grasping claws.

Mongolian Death Worm

The Mongolian Death Worm, also known as Allghoi Khorkhoi, was first sighted in 1926 in the Southern Gobi Desert in Mongolia. It is described as a thick-bodied worm between two and four feet long. It is reported to be able to spray an acid-like substance over large prey that causes death instantly. The creature is reported to hibernate during most of the year except for June and July when it becomes very active.

Morag

For centuries there have been reports of a creature dwelling in Loch Morar, just 70 miles from Loch Ness. The reports add further to the theory that some giant water-dwelling animals were living in the various lochs as they became land-locked thousands of years ago. Sightings of Morag have been numerous in the 20th century. In 1970, members of the Loch Ness

Investigation Bureau went to investigate the creature in Loch Morar. One member spotted a "hump-shaped object" unlike any normal marine life in the area.

Other Lake Monsters

Monsters have been reported in other lakes around the world, including the Irish Loughs of Ree and Fedda. On Norway's Lake Sudal, a huge creature with a head the size of a rowing boat has been sighted, while a giant red sea horse with a white mane, capable of speeds up to 70 mph, lurks in Storsjö Lake in Sweden. The monster Ogopogo haunts Canada's Lake Okanagan. New Brunswick, USA has the Lake Utopia Monster; Manipogo haunts Lake Manitoba in Canada; and the Lake Erie monster and the Flathead Lake Monster in Montana, USA, have all attained local fame, some of them long before Nessie came to the world's attention.

Mokele-Mbembe

Could a dinosaur still be alive today in the jungles of the Congo? Since 1913 there have been numerous sightings by local villagers of a creature that resembles a Brontosaurus. Foreigners like Professor Roy P. Mackal have also seen this animal in the Congo. It is about the size of an elephant, with short legs and a long neck. Mokele-Mbembe is herbivorous, but reportedly it has attacked humans.

Mothman

This creature was first spotted in 1966 in Point Pleasant, West Virginia, USA, after numerous UFO sightings. It is described as three to six feet tall, winged and headless, with glowing red eyes on its torso. Mothman has been seen flying across the sky at speeds of 100 mph. As it flies, it emits a high-pitched shriek.The deaths of several small animals and pets have been attributed to the monster.

Orang-Pendek

The Indonesian island of Sumatra is the home of the ape-like Orang-Pendek. It stands three to five feet tall, is covered with dark hair and has a bushy mane. It walks on the ground, and has a footprint like a human's. In 1989, British writer Deborah Martyr made casts of its footprints. The director of the Kerinci Selbat National Park said they were made by no animal he knew of. It is seen fairly often by locals, who say it lives off fruit and small animals.

Poltergeist

German for "knocking ghost", a poltergeist is a noisy supernatural spirit. They are supposed to move furniture, bang on walls and doors and break things to make their presence known. Poltergeists can be aggressive, hurling objects and striking people. They are said to turn up at séances, where they cause trouble.

Queensland Marsupial
This lion/tiger/cat is usually described as a heavy-set animal the size of a large dog with stripes across its back. It has a feline head and a nasty temperament, often taking its temper out on dogs sent out after it. Numerous reports describe it leaping through the air and disembowelling dogs with a swipe of its claws. Other reports indicate that it is a marsupial, with a peculiar hopping gait.

Zuiyo-maru Monster
On April 25, 1977, a fishing boat named the *Zuiyo-maru* was trawling east of Christchurch, New Zealand, when an enormous animal carcass became entangled in its nets. The massive creature, weighing about 20,000 pounds, was pulled aboard and photographed before being dumped back in the ocean. The beast, resembling a sea-going dinosaur, has yet to be identified.

MONSTERS OF THE DEEP

The Danger that Lurks Beneath

The Giant Squid

The existence of the Giant Squid is well accepted by science, though few have ever been seen, and little is known about its habits.

Giant Squid are carnivorous mollusks that have a long, torpedo-shaped body. At one end, surrounding a vicious beaked mouth strong enough to cut through steel cable, are five pairs of arms. One pair, longer than the rest, are used to catch food and bring it to the mouth. Just past the mouth are the eyes, the largest in the animal kingdom, measuring up to 18 inches across.

ROUND
1

The Giant Squid moves through the ocean using a jet of water forced out of its body by a siphon. It eats fish and other squid, and mounts terrifying attacks on whales and vessels at sea. The legends of the Kraken, a many-armed sea monster that could pull a whole ship under the water, are probably based on the Giant Squid.

The largest Giant Squid ever measured was discovered at Timble Tickle on November 2, 1878. The body was six yards from tail to beak. The longer tentacles measured over ten yards and were tipped with four-inch suckers.

In 1965, a Soviet whaling ship watched a battle between a Giant Squid and a 40 ton Sperm Whale. In this case neither was victorious. The strangled whale was found floating in the sea with the squid's

tentacles wrapped around its throat. The squid's severed head was found in the whale's stomach.

Sperm Whales eat squid, and originally it had been thought that fights between them were the result of a Sperm Whale taking on a squid that was just too large to be an easy meal. The incident with a ship, the *Brunswick* suggests otherwise ...

The *Brunswick* was an auxiliary tanker owned by the Royal Norwegian Navy. In the 1930s it was attacked at least three times by Giant Squid. In each case the squid would pull alongside, swim with the vessel, then suddenly turn and ram into the ship's side, wrapping its tentacles around the hull. The encounters were fatal for the squid. Unable to get a good grip on the ship's steel surface, the monsters slid off and fell into the ship's propellers to a grisly death.

Unfortunately for scientists, but good for the rest of us, humans do not meet up with Giant Squids very often, though there is at least one report from World War Two of survivors of a sunken naval vessel being attacked by a Giant Squid that ate one of the party.

Estimates based on damaged squid carcasses suggest these mighty monsters could reach up to 30 yards across. One story, though, suggests they might get even larger. One night during World War Two, a British Admiralty trawler was lying off the Maldive Islands in the Indian Ocean. One of the crew, A. G. Starkey, was up on deck, alone, fishing, when he saw something in the water.

"As I gazed, fascinated, a circle of green light glowed in my area of illumination. This green unwinking orb I suddenly realized was an eye. The surface of the water undulated with some strange disturbance. Gradually I realized that I was gazing at almost point-blank range at a huge squid." Starkey walked the length of the ship, finding the tail at one end and the tentacles at the other. The ship was over 50 yards long.

The Colossal Octopus

Known varieties of octopus range in size from a circumference of a few inches to as much as 15 feet. There is some evidence that, deep in the sea, there lives an unknown species of octopus that can grow to over 30 feet across and weigh ten tons.

The octopus is a distant cousin of the squid and both belong to a group of animals called cephalopods. Both are invertebrates, which means they have no backbone, and each has multiple arms, lined with suckers, that allow the creatures to hold fast to prey or other objects. Both are fairly intelligent, with large, dark eyes, and both are carnivorous.

Squid have ten arms, though, while the octopus – as its name suggests – has only eight. Squid are also thought to spend most of their time hovering in the mid-waters while the octopus lives on the ocean floor using its arms to move from rock to rock. Finally, while the squid has a reputation for aggression, the octopus has a more shy and retiring disposition. Only one (dead) Colossal Octopus has ever been found and it was, and still is, surrounded by controversy.

Not that octopi are entirely harmless. When angered, they can be dangerous to both

swimmers and divers. With their strong, long arms they can hold a man underwater until he drowns.

The story starts in November of 1896, when two boys, cycling along the beach in Florida, USA, came across the body of an enormous creature that had been washed up by the tide. Dr DeWitt Webb, a local amateur naturalist and president of the local historical society, took an interest in the remains. After an examination of the mutilated and decaying body, he believed that he'd discovered the carcass of a huge octopus.

The portion of the creature that remained – the body minus the arms – was five and a half yards in length and three yards wide. Parts of tentacles, unattached to the body, stretched as long as eleven yards with a diameter of

10 inches. Dr Webb estimated its weight at four or five tons.

Realising this was an important find, Webb wrote to Yale Professor Addison Verrill, a leading expert on cephalopods, about the creature:

"You may be interested to know of the body of an immense Octopus thrown ashore some miles south of this city. Nothing but the stump of the tentacles remains, as it had evidently been dead for some time before being washed ashore."

Based on photographs sent by Webb, Verrill concluded that the creature was indeed a Colossal Octopus that might have had a diameter of 45 yards when living.

Webb finally sent Verrill a sample of the tissue of the creature preserved in formalin.

Verrill was surprised to find it had the appearance of blubber and stated that he now believed the creature was a whale and that the arms were not associated with the body.

The whole matter would have rested like that if it hadn't been for Forrest Wood, the director of Marine Studios in Florida. Wood came across an old news story about the monster and discovered that Webb's sample was still stored at the Smithsonian Institution.

Wood persuaded the Smithsonian to let Dr Joseph Gennaro, of the University of Florida, to take some of the samples for analysis. Gennaro's examination under a microscope showed the tissue was more similar to octopus than whale or squid. Further tests later confirmed this. So it seems that Webb was right and

Verrill changed his mind too quickly. It may take another beached carcass to settle the matter.

A possible Colossal Octopus was recently found off New Zealand's Chatham Islands. The specimen, over four yards in length and weighing 160 pounds, was picked up in a trawler's net from a depth of 3,000 feet. The creature has been identified as *Haliphron Atlanticus* – a species of octopus never previously found in the area – by the National Institute of Water and Atmospheric Research.

Because the Colossal Octopus is a bottom dweller, it could be that when the creatures die they stay on the ocean floor and decay, leaving few clues for scientists to find. But as scientists explore the depths of the seas further, we may again come face to face with a Colossal Octopus and look into its huge unblinking eyes.

MONSTOGRAPHY

An A to Z of Mythical Monsters

Aigaumcha

A tiny African monster with eyes on its feet. The Aigaumcha's diet consists of human flesh.

Al

These Armenian monsters have iron teeth, brass claws and eat babies.

Ammut

This is an Egyptian monster with the head of a crocodile, a lion's body and the back end of a hippopotamus. The Egyptians call her the "eater of the dead", because that was her job in the Hall of Double Justice of the god Osiris. The hearts of the dead were weighed against the feather of truth and those that failed to past the test were fed to Ammut.

Banshee

The banshee in Irish Gælic is called "bean sidhe". In Scottish, "bean nighe", which means "supernatural woman". She is pictured with a sunken nose, untidy, wild hair and huge, hollow eye sockets. A bean nighe has one prominent tooth, one nostril, long, hanging breasts, and webbed feet. Her eyes are fiery red from continuous weeping. She wears a tattered white sheet and cloak flapping around her, and wails loudly outside the door of someone who is about to die.

Basilisk

A small but deadly reptile, only 6 inches long, whose breath is poisonous. In ancient legend was said to possess a glance that would turn any person instantly to stone.

Bobbi-Bobbi

One of the ancestral snakes of the Binbinga people of northern Australia, Bobbi-Bobbi once sent a number of flying foxes (large bats) for hungry men to eat, but they escaped. So the snake, watching from his underground home, threw one of his own ribs up to the men, who used it as a boomerang to kill the bats; then they cooked them. Later, however, they used the boomerang to make a hole in the sky. This angered the snake, and he snatched back his rib. Two men who tried to hang on to it were dragged underground and eaten alive.

Centaur

The most famous centaurs are those from Greek mythology. In these myths, the centaurs are a race of creatures that are half-man and half-horse. The father of the original centaurs is the god, Ixion. There are many variations of the centaur. Some have a human torso and head on a horse's body. Some are entire humans with a horse's body and hind legs stretching back from the waist. Another variation gives the centaur wings, and sometimes the centaur's head has horsey ears.

Cerberus

The fearsome three-headed dog of Greek legend who guards the entrance to Hell, Cerberus has a serpent's tail, and is also known as the "Hound of Hades". The mighty Hercules is the only person ever to best him in combat, bringing him back up with him to the world of men for a time, as one of his Twelve Labors.

Cyclops

A man-eating giant who has one eye in the middle of his forehead. In Greek mythology, the Cyclops captured the hero Odysseus, who escaped after he put out the Cyclops' eye.

Dagon

The ancient Philistines, and later the seafaring Phoenicians, considered this half-man half-fish to be their main god. In the Bible it tells that while conquering the Israelites, the Philistines stole the Ark of the Covenant and placed it before a statue of Dagon. This shape-shifting marine god may date back to the ancient Sumerian god, Oannes, who came from the ocean to educate mankind.

Damballah
The powerful serpent god of voodoo myth, he shows himself in the sky above Haiti, in the Caribbean, appearing with his wife, Ayida, as a rainbow.

Dragon (Western)
Native Americans believed in snake dragons: enormous, fire-breathing serpents with scaly green bodies and huge red wings. Greedy creatures, they hoard treasure in dens under the earth. Fierce and hungry, a dragon is partial to young human flesh. Dragons live in caves, mountains, or lakes. They were particularly active in the Middle Ages in Europe, when brave knights challenged them in battle.

Dragon (Eastern)

Compared to Western dragons, these beasts are quite small. Their bodies are long, and they have two horns for ears. They have no wings, and their soft breath is said to form clouds. They do not roar; instead they make the sounds of beating gongs and jingling bells. Chinese dragons dine on sparrows. They live wherever there is water. They are kind and wise friends of human beings. At Chinese New Year, dancers don huge dragon costumes and perform special dances in the streets.

Dzoavits

A huge ogre from the myths of the Shoshoneans – a primitive people of Nevada and Utah in the USA. It was conquered by a badger, who lured the mighty giant to a specially prepared hole, threw hot rocks in on him, and then plugged the hole with a boulder, trapping him inside.

Erlking

Erlking is a Germanic goblin who is King of the dwarves. He lures humans, especially children, to the forest and kills them.

Fachen

The Fachen is a monster from Irish legend. He is known to chase and attack travellers, eventually killing them. He is covered with feathers, including a tuft on his head like that of a cockerel. He has one mangled hand that grows from the middle of his chest, and one leg that grows out of his body. He also has one eye set in the middle of his forehead.

Ga-Gorib

In Hottentot myth, this monster would sit on the edge of a great pit and dare passers-by to throw stones at him. The stone always rebounded and killed the thrower, who then fell into the pit to be devoured.

Giant

Albanian giants are as tall as pine trees, with long, black beards. They catch men to eat and women to fan the flies away.

Giants have enormous size and strength packed in a human form. They can roar like thunder, make the earth shake, and snack on grown people. Their characteristics depend on their nationalities. Irish giants are pleasant, English giants are openly evil, and Welsh giants are clever and cunning (for giants). All giants have a keen sense of smell, and use it to sniff out their next victim. Usually their brains are no match for their bodies and they can be outwitted by a smart human. Giants are proof that intelligence is more important than size.

Giantess

Scottish giantesses are known as gruagachs, like their male counterparts. Like most female giants, they are depicted as housewife types who spend their time making bread out of ground-up human bones. Befri, a French giantess, carried off young girls and made them spin thread into cloth. Grendel's mother, in the Norse story of Beowulf, was a mighty ogress who sneaked up on sleeping warriors and ate them 15 at a time.

Goblin

From their birthplace in France, these nasty cousins of gnomes have spread all over Europe. When they entered England in ancient times, the Druids called them Robin Goblins, from which the name "hobgoblin" derives. Goblins have no permanent home, living in old trees and under moss-covered rocks. Playful on occasion, goblins are nonetheless to be avoided. A goblin's smile can curdle blood, and its laugh can turn milk sour. Goblins amuse themselves by hiding things, spilling food, and confusing travellers by changing signposts.

MILK

Gorgons

In Greek mythology, the Gorgons were the three daughters of Phorkys and Keto. Their names were Stheino, Euryale and (the most famous) Medusa. They had wings and claws, and snakes instead of hair. Medusa had the power to turn men to stone simply by looking them in the eyes. When she was slain by Perseus, the legendary winged horse Pegasus rose from her fresh blood.

Gnome

The word "gnome" comes from the Greek "gnosis" meaning "knowledge". It was said that they knew where to find precious metals. They are depicted as grotesque dwarves wearing tight-fitting brown clothes and hoods. They live underground and guard the Earth's treasures. Sometimes they are confused with goblins, but gnomes are good-natured, hard-working and reliable, whereas goblins are nasty and spiteful.

Gremlin

Gremlins were born in the United States. Highly mechanical, they have been responsible for much technological progress. They live around tools and inside machines and appliances. During World War Two, however, gremlins turned against mankind, after human mechanics and scientists began to take credit for gremlin work. They started to cause mechanical failures in aircrafts, motor vehicles and other mechanical devices, and gremlins are blamed for technical glitches of all kinds to this day.

Harpies

The Harpies were loathsome monsters employed by the gods to punish crime on Earth. They were three sisters with the bodies of birds and the heads of women, with trunks like elephants. Always ravenous, they would punish wrongdoers by stealing their food and leaving them to starve.

Hippogryph

The hippogryph is a cross between a male gryphon and a filly. It has the head, wings and front legs of a gryphon, and the body and hind legs of a horse. It is a powerful creature that can move through the air with astonishing speed. It figured in several of the legends of Charlemagne as a mount for some of his knights.

Ichthyocentaur

The Ichthyocentaur is a variation of the centaur. Living in the sea, it has the upper half of a man, the tail of a dolphin and the forelegs of a horse or lion.

Jinshin-uwo

The source of all Japanese earthquakes, this thousand-yard-long eel carries Japan on its back. By lashing its large tail, the Jinshin-uwo, or "earthquake fish", causes the ground above to rumble and shake.

Kappa
An ugly green monster from Japan with a monkey's head and a turtle's shell, it drags people into its watery home to eat them.

Leprechaun
Leprechauns are small fairies from Irish folklore. Grotesque in appearance, dressed in green with leather aprons, silver-buckled shoes, red caps, and spectacles on the end of their noses, leprechauns are famous for being shoemakers. But a leprechaun will never make a pair of shoes: he will make just one shoe at a time. They like to play tricks on humans but if a leprechaun is caught by a human (which is very difficult to accomplish), he is forced to reveal the location of his hidden treasure, usually gold. While he is guiding you to his treasure, you must watch him very closely – if you take your eyes off him for a single second, he will vanish into thin air.

Lernaean Hydra

A fearsome beast from Greek mythology with nine heads, whose very breath and smell is deadly poison to mortal men. Eight of the Hydra's heads are mortal; the ninth is impossible to kill.

Kraken

The Kraken, which is found in Scandinavian myth, is a huge sea creature. It is said to lie at the bottom of the sea for long periods of time and then surface, when sailors mistake the creature's many humps for a chain of small islands, sometimes even landing on one and building a camp, only to be drowned when the creature submerges once more. The Kraken is supposed to have enormous tentacles, which can seize even the largest ships and drag them, and all on board, to a watery grave.

Logaroo

Like vultures by day, these mythical Caribbean creatures shed their skin at night, hide in fog, and suck blood from the lost victims they catch.

Lung

The rainbringing dragons of Chinese folklore. The Lung were called upon in ancient times to refresh the Earth with their waters. The Lung can make themselves as small as silkworms, or become so large that they can overshadow the entire world. They are composed of many parts of different animals. The horns of a stag sit on the head of a camel, with the eyes of a demon and the neck of a snake. They are covered in the scales of a fish, and have the claws of an eagle, the pads of a tiger, the ears of a bull and the whiskers of a cat.

Manticora
From the West Indies, the Manticora is a lion with human features and eyes that burn blue fire; it can shoot deadly quills from its tail.

Minotaur
A half-man half-bull monster from the island of Crete, the Minotaur is the son of the Queen, Pasiphae, and a bull sent to her by the sea god, Poseidon. Her husband, Minos, built a labyrinth (maze) on the island to contain his monstrous stepson. The Minotaur, usually pictured as having a human body and a bull's head, ate human flesh. It was sent seven boys and seven girls every year as a sacrifice, to stop it from leaving Crete to terrorize the world at large.

New Jersey Devil
An American monster that is part ram, part kangaroo with bat wings, a horse's feet, and a pointed tail. It feeds on barnyard animals.

Nixie

Nixies are Germanic sprites who live in water. Although the male doesn't often show himself to humans, the female is often seen sitting in the sun on the banks of rivers and lakes. Nixie maidens are beautiful with long hair and blue eyes. If a man tries to spy on their beauty, their song can cause him to go mad.

O Goncho

A dragon from Japan. Every 50 years this white beast turns into a golden bird. Its cry signifies the coming of famine.

Oni

The Oni are Japanese demons. In Shinto legend, they are associated with disease, calamity and misfortune. These interfering spirits are basically human in shape, but possess three eyes, a wide mouth, horns, and three sharp talons on both hands and feet. Oni can fly, often swooping down to seize the soul of a wicked man who is about to die.

Ovda

An unfriendly forest spirit, Ovda wanders in the woods of Finland as a naked human being with its feet turned backwards. Sometimes it appears as a man, sometimes a woman. Ovda entices its victims by challenging them to dance; then it tickles them to death.

Ping Feng

A huge, pig-like beast from China, Ping Feng has a head at each end, and attacks people and large animals.

Pixie

No larger than a human hand, a pixie is human-like with red hair and green eyes. They have upturned noses and mischievous smiles. They wear tight-fitting green clothes. Pixies can change their size at will. They are tricksters who like to lead humans astray, and are usually found in the English counties of Somerset, Devon, and Cornwall.

Some farmers embrace the presence of pixies and do certain things to keep them on the farm, leaving a bucket of water out so mother pixies can wash their babies, and milk for them to drink. They will also sweep the hearth so that the pixies have a clean place to dance.

Questing Beast

The Questing Beast has a snake's head, a leopard's body and a lion's back end with the paws of a hare, or a deer's hooves. It is continually seeking water to slake its unquenchable thirst. As it runs, its belly makes the sound of a pack of hounds. It appears several times in the legends of King Arthur.

Rakshasa

An ogre who lives in a palace in India. His gold and jewels make him rich, but he is filthy and quite stupid. Like all ogres, he enjoys eating people. He can appear in many ugly shapes, coming from nowhere to kill his victims with a single scratch from his poisonous tail.

Redcap

Redcaps are malevolent goblins, easily distinguishable by their red hats and fiery red eyes. Their caps are red because they dip them in the blood of their human victims. Redcaps wear iron boots, but are quick on their feet. They live in castles along the English-Scottish border. They have sharp eagle's talons with which they kill their victims. Short and stocky, redcaps have long white beards and look like old men. Just as with goblins, all that is needed to keep them at bay is the use of certain well-chosen holy words.

Sasabonsam

A monster from Ashanti myth, the Sasabonsam is a hairy beast with large, bloodshot eyes, long legs and feet pointing both ways. Its favorite trick is to sit in the high branches of a tree and dangle its long legs, so as to entrap unwary hunters.

Scorpion Men

From ancient Sumerian legend, Scorpion Men are born of the god Tiamat along with the viper, dragon, sphinx, great lion and mad dog. They are human from the waist up and scorpion from the waist down. The astrological constellation, Scorpio, comes from this creature. It was often depicted as a guard in the city of Babylon.

Tiamat

The dreaded dragon of Babylonian legend, Tiamat was said to be revolting in appearance, being a cross between a bird, a serpent and an animal, and she was seen as utterly evil. Tiamat was eventually defeated by the god, Marduk, who shot a raging wind into her mouth, so that she could not close it and swallow him, then shot an arrow into her belly, slaying her. Marduk then created the heavens and Earth out of her dead body.

Sleipnir

In Viking mythology, this horse was the steed of the god Odin (from whom we get the word Wednesday). This grey horse had eight legs and could run faster than the wind. It could fly in the air, run on the earth and dive down into the regions of hell.

Troll

In Norse mythology, trolls are known as dim-witted gigantic man-eating creatures who live in caves in the mountains. They are ugly and quite evil. Trolls would be turned to stone if they were hit by the sun's rays. They guard treasure and are good at metal-working. In later legends, trolls are smaller, dwarf-like beings who still live in caves but are not as strong or bloodthirsty as their predecessors. They still like to steal women and children, though, and are cleverer than their forefathers.

Unicorn

The first mention of the unicorn came from the Roman Ctesias in 389 BC: he said that it was a wild beast similar to a horse. Pure in spirit, with white bodies, red heads and blue eyes, unicorns have a single ivory horn on their heads.

Wishpoosh

According to the Nez Perce Indians of Washington, the beaver monster Wishpoosh refused to allow anyone to fish. Whenever a person came to the lake where he lived, he would seize them with his huge claws and drag them underwater.

Wyvern

Appearing quite often in heraldry, the Wyvern is a snake-like dragon with wings. It has two legs with talons like an eagle and a tail that ends in a point like an arrowhead. The Wyvern symbolizes war, pestilence, envy and viciousness.

Yuki Onna

The Yuki Onna, or Snow Woman, is a Japanese female demon that inhabits snowstorms and causes travellers to become lost. Eventually the weary trekkers become exhausted and freeze to death.

Ziz

A bird mentioned in the book of Psalms in the Bible, the Ziz is a bird of enormous size. It can block out the sun with its wings and has incredible strength. It is said that it was created to protect all small birds, and without its protection, these birds would have died a long time ago. When roasted, it is also said to be a delicacy for gigantic banquets.

Zombie

Followers of some branches of Haitian and West African voodoo believe a spirit or spell can bring a corpse back to life to perform evil deeds for its master. These are zombies: they walk like robots and can be made to do anything for their masters, from manual labor to murder.

FANGS FOR THE MEMORY

A Brief History of Vampires

In 1047, the first appearance of the word "upir" (an early form of the word which later became "vampire") was in a document referring to a Russian prince as "upir lichy", or "wicked vampire".

In around 1250**, several suspected cases of vampirism were reported in the East European country of Moravia, now part of the Czech Republic. Reports circulated that a vampire was leaving its tomb in the local cemetery and attacking sleeping women and children. Those who had seen the vampire said it was a leading citizen of the community who had recently died. A "vampire hunter" was summoned from neighboring Hungary.**

The story goes that the vampire hunter climbed up the church tower overlooking the cemetery and kept watch. When the man saw the vampire emerge from his tomb and disappear into the town, he hurried down and stole a shroud from the open coffin. When the vampire returned and found its shroud missing, it looked up at the tower which the hunter had reclimbed and began to howl with an unearthly voice. The man challenged the creature to come up the tower and retrieve its shroud. The vampire hunter kept his nerve until the creature had almost reached him, then knocked it off the building with a shovel. Before the vampire could recover from the fall, the man descended and cut off its head with the shovel.

In 1310, King Philip of France ordered that the corpse of a certain Jehan de Turo be dug up and destroyed by fire "on suspicion that he was a vampire".

In 1451, **at Gratz in the mountainous regions of upper Styria, now a province of Austria, lived Barbara de Cilly, a beautiful woman much loved by one Sigismund of Hungary. When close to death, her life was apparently saved by a secret ritual devised by Abramerlin the Mage, but as a result was condemned forever after to be a vampire. She became the inspiration for** *Camilla*, **a vampire novel by the Irish writer, Joseph Sheridan Le Fanu.**

In 1560, Elizabeth Bathory, later known as the "Blood Countess", was born. She was arrested in 1610 for killing several hundred people and bathing in their blood. Tried and convicted, she was sentenced to life imprisonment. She was bricked into a room in her castle, where she died in 1614.

In 1734, **the word "vampyre" entered the English language after German accounts of waves of vampire hysteria. In 1798, Samuel Taylor Coleridge wrote** *Christabel*, **now believed to be the first vampire poem in English.**

In 1810, reports circulated through northern England of sheep being killed by having their jugular veins cut and their blood drained.

In 1819, **Dr John Polidori's** *The Vampyre*, **the first vampire story in English, was published in** *New Monthly Magazine*. **It was entered for the same writing competition for which Mary Shelley wrote** *Frankenstein*, **and its central character, Lord Ruthven, was modelled after the famous poet Lord Byron. Many were convinced Byron had penned the tale himself, based on his own vampiric experiences.**

In 1845, after the death of Horace Ray in Jewett City, Connecticut, USA, the members of his family all fell ill with a wasting disease. When just one sickly son remained alive, the father's body was dug up from its grave and found to be as fresh as the day it had been laid to rest. After the corpse was burned, the health of the surviving son improved and he lived to a ripe old age, convinced that his dad had indeed been a vampire.

In 1872, **in Italy, Vincenzo Verzeni was convicted of murdering two people and drinking their blood.**

In 1897, Bram Stoker's novel, *Dracula*, revived the story of Vlad the Impaler for the modern world. Considered by many scholars to be the most bloodthirsty full-length book in English literature, it has never gone out of print and remains a bestseller. Sadly, Stoker never lived to see *Dracula's* phenomenal success. He died in 1912, a poor and unrecognized man.

Also in 1897, **another novel, entitled** *The Vampire,* **created in detail the vampire character we recognize on stage and in hundreds of movies ever since. It was written by Rudyard Kipling, who also wrote the book on which the Disney movie** *The Jungle Book* **was based.**

In 1921, the remains of a suspected vampire were found in Essex, England. A skeleton believed to be that of a woman, which was found in St Osyth, is thought to have been buried as a vampire. As custom decreed, the remains had been bound with rope, and nails had been driven through the thigh bones to prevent it from rising from the grave after death.

In 1958, **Hammer Films in Great Britain started a new wave of interest in vampires with the first of its** *Dracula* **films.**

In 1964, *The Munsters* and *The Addams Family* – two horror comedies with vampire characters – were first shown on American TV.

In 1992, **Andrei Chikatilo of Rostov, Russia, was sentenced to death after killing and "vampirizing" 55 people.**

In 1996, members of a vampire cult led by Rod Ferrell were arrested for the murder of two people in Florida, USA. They were subsequently tried and convicted of the murders.

In 1997, **celebrations marked a hundred years since the publication of Bram Stoker's novel** *Dracula*. **These led to Dracula-related books, TV shows and the release of commemorative postage stamps in Canada, Ireland, England and the United States.**

UNLUCKY DIP

Miscellaneous Monstrosities

After Nelson's death at the Battle of Trafalgar in 1805, his body is thought to have been preserved in a barrel of rum or brandy for the trip home

The ghost of a famous Japanese samurai warrior named Masakado Taira has his own bank account worth more than $200,000. Although Taira died 1,000 years ago, Tokyo residents still leave food, gifts and money at his stone monument located in the heart of the city's financial district. Managing Taira's funds, and everything else related to the spirit, is a man called Tatsuzo Endo, chairman of the Masakado Preservation Society, who admits, "I'm not really sure ghosts need money."

The word "Pokemon" is an abbreviation of "pocket monster". In Japan the word "poke" is used to mean something small. The video game was launched in 1996 in Japan by Satoshi Tajira, and the craze spread to trading cards, comic books, a television series, films and toys, with sales running into billions of dollars. Officially there were only 150 species of Pokemon, but unknown to the manufacturers, Nintendo, Tajira hid a 151st in the software, the rare and powerful Mew.

Frankenstein's castle actually exists. It is located in Darmstadt in Germany. But the mad scientist who lived there and performed the experiments wasn't a Dr Frankenstein, but one Konrad Johann Dippel. He occupied the castle in the 17th century, using corpses from the local cemetery to experiment on. When the townspeople started to suspect him

of stealing corpses, he stopped using them and started trying the experiments on himself. He later died after drinking one of his own potions.

The Tibetans used to have a novel way of keeping their lamas, or spiritual leaders, with them after death. First, the body of the departed was packed with lacquer-saturated padding. Then it was wrapped in lacquered silk and placed in a seated position in a hot room filled with salt. After several days of drying, it was cooled down, then covered all over with gold leaf and placed on a throne with the other gilded lamas.

The Ancient Incas of Peru preserved dead bodies with a combination of aromatic oils and slow drying.

Alexander the Great's body was preserved in honey.

When St John of the Cross died in 1591, he was buried in a vault beneath the floor of a church in Ubeda, Spain. When the tomb was opened nine months later, his body was said to be fresh and intact; and when a finger was removed to use as a holy relic, it bled like that of a living person. The body was exhumed again in 1859, and again said to be in perfect condition, 250 years after his death.

In Haiti, the poison found in the glands of puffer fish is used in a powder for making "zombies". It brings on a state of paralysis so complete that although the person is alive, they seem dead, even to a doctor. The puffer fish is also eaten in Japan as a very expensive delicacy, carved by chefs specially trained to ensure no poison is left on the diner's plate. Mistakes do occur however, and people still die every year from eating this dangerous treat.

"Teratophobia" is the fear of monsters.

A person born on Halloween is reputedly able to see and talk to spirits.

Vampire bats don't suck blood. They make a small incision in an animal's skin and lap up the oozing blood with their tongues.

In East Africa, soccer teams hire witch doctors to ensure their success. Known as "jujumen", these soothsaying specialists use a variety of magical rituals to create successful outcomes for their teams. In fact, witchcraft is considered part of the team's mental preparation for a game; just knowing that a jujuman is using divine powers helps team members relax. Typical witchcraft prescriptions include avoiding women first thing in the morning and leaving soccer balls on a grave during the night before a big game.

If you fancy following in the footsteps of the ancient Egyptians and becoming a mummy after your own death, you can. Summum, a religious group in Salt Lake City, Utah, USA, will do the mummification for $63,000. The modern technique involves being soaked for six months in a secret formula of preservation fluid, dozens of coats of polyurethane rubber, and layers of fibreglass bandages. Your mummified body is then sealed into a bronze case with resin, pharoah-style.

In 1982, *Empire* magazine published a letter written by a woman from Colorado, USA. She claimed that in 1935, when she was a young child, she saw five baby dinosaurs. A few months after she saw them a farmer shot one. The woman saw the body, and said it was "about seven feet tall, was grey, had a head like a snake, short front legs with claws that resembled chicken feet, large stout back legs, and a long tail."

Before becoming the most famous Frankenstein's Monster on our movie screens, actor Boris Karloff was an estate agent.

Traditionally, individuals with a natural squint, as well as dwarfs and hunchbacks, are considered to have the evil-eye: able to cause harm to victims just with a look. Curiously, in Mediterranean lands, blue-eyed folks are more likely to be accused of possessing an evil stare, while in northern Europe, dark-eyed people are more suspect.

The infamous Black Death in Europe was due in part to the fact that people believed cat owners to be witches. All the cats were rounded up, caged and burned, leaving the rats (with their disease-causing parasites) to run free and multiply. Those secretly harboring cats were among the ones who survived.

In the Trang area of Thailand, locals believe that evil spirits are causing a stream of fatal car accidents. The troubled stretch of road is known as the "100 corpses crossroads" and has created commotion and concern all the way to the highest levels of government. One Thai politician has asked for local monks to conduct a religious ceremony to help improve safety. Spirits of the dead victims are also being asked to help guard the area.

Some people believe that objects that have been in contact with each other have a psychic link, and that their personal possessions will forever be psychically joined with them. That's why a witch is extra-anxious when a personal belonging goes missing: she's fearful that the item that once touched her body could be used in a nasty spell against her.

According to ancient tradition, to protect your home from evil spirits on Halloween, you must walk around your house three times backwards and anti-clockwise before sunset.

Beneath the streets of Paris lie catacombs of bones. Six million people are buried there, their bones arranged as walls. Skulls are arranged as crosses, and form entire archways. Trips through the mass graves have been on offer to brave tourists.

In Thailand, the bodies of monks are preserved in the belief that the purity of their souls in life has assured that their earthly remains are pure. These monks are on public display and are objects of worship. No special techniques are said to be used to preserve the bodies, yet they decay very slowly even in an atmosphere of smog, humidity, and heat. They still have teeth, hair, and skin, decades after their deaths.

PART 3

MONSTER GAMES & STORIES

SPOOKY!

Eerie Episodes

John William Dunne believed time travel was possible. At the age of 31, he was involved in designing and building the first British military aircraft. Dunne also kept an extensive log of his dreams, which he believed could tell the future. Astonishingly, one dream correctly predicted a volcanic disaster on the island of Martinique in which 40,000 people were killed.

A sixteen-year-old boy worked on his grandfather's horse farm. One morning he drove a pickup truck into town on an errand. While he was walking along main street, he suddenly saw Death: black cloak, hooded, glowing red eyes. Death beckoned him close with a bony finger. Terrified, the boy drove back to the farm as fast as he could and told his grandfather what had happened.

"Lend me the truck," he begged. "I'll go to the city. He won't find me there!"

His grandfather lent him the truck, and the boy sped away. After he left, his grandfather went into town looking for Death. When he found him, he asked, "Why did you frighten my grandson that way? He is only sixteen. He is too young to die."

"I am sorry about that," said Death. "I did not mean to beckon to him. But I was surprised to see him here. I have an appointment with him this afternoon in the city."

Mr Brand was elderly and poorly, and during his last days, there was nothing his wife and the doctors could do for him, except make him as comfortable as possible until he passed away. One night, Mrs Brand saw

headlights speeding up the driveway to their home. "Oh no," she thought, "I don't want visitors now, not now."

But it wasn't a car bringing a visitor. It was an old hearse with maybe a half dozen little men hanging from the sides. At least, that's what it looked like.

The hearse screeched to a stop. The men jumped off and stared up at her, their eyes glowing with a soft yellow light, like cats' eyes.

She watched with horror as they disappeared into a side door of her house. An instant later they were back outside, lifting something into the hearse. Then they drove off at high speed, wheels squealing, the gravel in the driveway flying in all directions.

At that very moment, the nurse came in, put her hand on Mrs Brand's shoulder, and told her that her husband had died.

On Halloween night, 1975, a handsome stranger walked into the El Camaroncito Nite Club off Old Highway 90, near San Antonio. He was a brilliant dancer and even the shyest girl in the room couldn't resist his request for a turn around the floor.

One partner was almost in a trance as she whirled and spun with the man, and the crowd watched, enraptured. Suddenly his partner cried out in terror: "Your feet! Your feet!" She screamed, and tore herself from his tight embrace.

Horrified patrons looked down and saw long, skinny claws protruding from the stranger's trousers. He had chicken's feet, a sign of the devil. Other women began to scream hysterically and say prayers. The stranger walked into the men's cloakroom and disappeared – leaving behind only a strong smell of sulphur – the devil's scent.

In 1979, American David Booth had a series of recurring nightmares of a plane crashing, and on May 25, 1979, his premonitions came true.

A DC-10 took off from Chicago's O'Hare Airport, flew half a mile, then turned on its side and slammed into the ground, exploding on impact. The 272 passengers and crew on board all perished.
Booth's dreams started on May 16, and after they had continued for seven nights – having clearly seen in his dreams the name of the airline involved in the accident – he went and told people in authority at the airport.

They made notes of what he'd told them, and showed genuine concern, but claimed they couldn't just ground a whole airline. So the planes went on as usual – and David Booth's nightmares came true.

A young man and his wife were on a road trip to visit his mother. It was getting dark, so he decided to look for a place to stay overnight; they could finish the journey in the morning.

Just off the road, they saw a small house in the woods. So they stopped to ask if a room was available to rent. An elderly man and woman came to the door. It wasn't a motel, they said, but they would be glad to have them stay as their guests. They had plenty of room and would enjoy the company.

The old woman made coffee, brought out some cake, and the four of them talked for a while. Then the young couple were shown to a nice bedroom. They explained to the old couple that they wanted to pay them something for their kindness, but the old man insisted he would not accept any money.

The young couple got up early next morning before their hosts had awakened. On a table near the front door, they left an envelope with some money in it for the room.

They went on to the next town, stopping at a restaurant for breakfast. When they told the owner where they had stayed, he was confused. "That can't be," he said. "That house burned to the ground ten years ago, the old man and woman who lived there died in the fire."

The young couple could not believe it. They went back to the house, only to find that indeed, it wasn't there. All they found was a burned-out shell. They stared at the ruins trying to understand what had happened.

And strangest of all, in the rubble was a badly burned table and on it was the envelope they had left there that morning.

THE UNEXPLAINED

Truth is Stranger than Fiction

"Clairaudience" is the ability to hear voices from the dead. The most famous example in history is that of Joan of Arc, the French heroine who claimed to have heard supernatural voices urging her to aid her countrymen in the fight against the English army. The English burned her at the stake.

The captain of the Argentine ship *Keweah* was interviewed by the New York Times regarding a "strange and monstrous animal" he had seen on the Patagonian coast in 1906. He said that when he was looking towards the shore, he "heard a sound and saw a huge, ice-covered boulder splash into the sea from the high, rocky shore." At the spot where the boulder had been dropped from, he said there stood an animal with a head like a hound and a 30-foot-long neck.

Outside the town of Gold Hill Oregon, there is a place that has baffled visitors and professional investigators alike.

Nestled in the forest is the Oregon Vortex. Since 1930, visitors the world over have gone to this area of mystical energy where bottles roll uphill, broomsticks stand up by themselves, and people seem to grow and shrink by moving just a couple of steps.

Native American tribes knew of this place long before the white people came there. Animals wouldn't enter it, so they avoided it, naming it "The Forbidden Land".
If photographs are taken in the Vortex, mist- like forms appear on the prints, and balls of light appear in the pictures.
Even stranger, planes flying over the area suffer malfunctions in their instruments, suggesting the Vortex powers stretch way above the ground.

According to a report in *The Times* newspaper, women hanging clothes up to dry in Cupar, Scotland in June of 1842 were said to have heard a sudden explosion, and watched as the clothes shot up into the sky. Some of the clothing did fall back to the ground, but others kept ascending until they disappeared. Oddly, the clothes were carried off to the north, but the wind was blowing to the south that day.

One evening in the summer of 1849, the *Edinburgh New Philosophical Journal* reported "a curious phenomenon" at Balvullich farm. There was a clap of thunder, and "a large and irregularly shaped mass of ice" 20 feet wide crashed to earth. "It had a beautiful crystalline appearance, being nearly all quite transparent, composed of small diamond-shapes, all firmly congealed together." Today, it would be put down to ice falling from an aircraft ... but in 1849? In summer?

Rock fans know "Foo Fighters" as the name of a band headed by former Nirvana member Dave Grohl. During World War Two, British, American and even German fighter pilots were plagued by weird balls of light that flew in circles around their planes. They called them "Foo Fighters". Although their true origin has never been found, both the Allies and the Nazis believed the lights were a secret weapon possessed by the other side. The catch-phrase of a cartoon character of the time, named Smokey Stover, was: "Where there's foo, there's fire." The phrase was adopted to describe the phenomenon.

During a rainstorm near Boring, Oregon, in 1911, a woman out walking felt large objects hitting her head and shoulders. She looked up to see hundreds of salamanders "falling from the sky, literally covering the ground and wriggling and crawling all over".

Michelle Jessett of Glynneath, Wales, suffered from a mysterious malady that had doctors perplexed. Incredibly, when Michelle cried, acid-like tears burned her face and blistered her skin. According to her parents, Michelle once breathed in fumes when a truck carrying chemicals overturned and burned. Afterwards she dropped out of school and visited the hospital more than 30 times, complaining that her tears left a fiery trail down her cheeks.

A Dutch study recently presented evidence of the existence of the human soul. Doctors interviewing 344 heart-attack survivors found that ten per cent of them felt emotions, visions or thoughts when they were clinically dead. Some had "out-of-body" experiences, looking down upon their own bodies and hearing the conversations of people in the room. These experiences have been offered as proof that the soul has a life outside the physical body.

TOO GROSS FOR COMFORT

Yucky Yarns

A family was given a gift of a huge cactus. They gave it a place of honor in the dining room, and soon noticed a strange phenomenon – it appeared to be breathing! In and out, in and out, ever so slightly the sides of the huge plant were moving. The mother decided to check it out with the local botanical society, and she gave them a ring. She described the "breathing" to the cactus expert at the society, who gasped and told the mother to "GET IT OUT OF THE HOUSE NOW!" She dropped the phone and ran to get the plant out into the garden. As soon as she got it outside, the cactus exploded and 20,000 scorpions spilled out all over the lawn!

In West Yorkshire, England, Elaine Sheridan was preparing to feed her three dogs from a tin of dog food when a live toad jumped out of the tin and across her kitchen floor. According to animal expert Dr Roger Meek, the toad could have survived the three months it had spent canned by shutting down its metabolism. The Sheridans kept the lucky toad as a pet and named it Buddy after the toads from the Budweiser beer commercials.

Two elderly women went shopping. As they came out of the mall they spied a dead cat in the car park. Being cat lovers, they couldn't bear the thought of leaving the poor dead kitty there. They decided to take it home and give it a decent burial. They went back into the store and got some shopping bags. They wrapped the dead kitty in one bag and then put it in another bag, hoping to contain the stink ... *(Continued on next page.)*

It was lunch-time so their next stop was a local restaurant. As it was a warm day, they were reluctant to leave the dead kitty closed up in the car. So they placed the bag beside their car and went in to eat.

Their car was visible through the window where they were sitting. They watched, amazed, as a lady walked by their car, stopped, went back, stole their shopping bag, and walked into the restaurant!

The thief ordered her lunch, and, curiosity getting the better of her, she opened the bag and peeked inside. She then screamed, fell and hit her head, knocking herself out. An ambulance was called to take the poor woman away. As they were carrying her off, one of the elderly cat lovers placed the shopping bag on the stretcher, saying, "I think this belongs to her ..."

The Parsi community of Zoroastrians in Bombay, India follow an ancient religion, founded in 600 B.C. They believe that human remains can't be buried, cremated or disposed of at sea.

Instead, the Zoroastrians leave their dearly departed on top of tall stone towers, open to the sky, called the "Towers of Silence", so that vultures can eat the corpses as they dry in the sun. Unfortunately, the vultures in Bombay have become nearly extinct over the past decade, and the Parsi community is struggling to find a solution to their disposal problem, as an average of 900 members of their religion pass away each year.

The mostly non-Parsi residents of the homes around the Towers of Silence are becoming increasingly offended by the smell of rotting corpses in the locality, and would like the towers to be moved.

Marc Quinn creates works of art using an unusual choice of material – his own blood. One of his best-known pieces is a sculpture of his own head made out of his blood that has been frozen solid. He used nine pints of blood for the sculpture, which created a sensation when it was first exhibited. The life-sized blood-red head even caused some people to faint when they saw it.

Unfortunately, the work is no longer with us. The sculpture was purchased by millionaire art collector Charles Saatchi, who kept it in his home in a refrigerated case. Workmen in Saatchi's home moved the freezer case, unplugging the motor that kept the freezer going. A little later, the workers noticed that a pool of liquid had formed around the floor.

They opened the freezer lid, and saw to their horror that the fragile, irreplaceable work of art was now a puddle of blood.

A man found his dog in the garden with a piece of dirty fur in its mouth. A closer look proved that the fur was actually a prize rabbit belonging to the neighbors. It was very dead, but with no obvious injuries.

The man was horrified. He quickly took the rabbit inside, shampooed and blow-dried it, then snuck next door to put it back in the hutch before his neighbor got home.

A few days went by and he heard nothing. Then at the weekend he was talking over the fence to his neighbor, who said a bizarre thing had happened that week. He had came home from work one night to found his prize rabbit dead in its hutch. "Oh, no," said the man. "How awful!"

"That's not it," said the neighbor. "What's weird is that it had died earlier that morning and I buried it before I left for work!"

TERRIFYING TALES

Seriously Scary Stories

A nurse named Jane was unable to get along with the other nurses in her hospital. She was bitchy, unkind, and constantly quarrelling with people. One night after Jane had been particularly horrible to a young student nurse, a bunch of colleagues decided to do something to teach her a lesson.

One of the nurses on surgery duty agreed to bring a patient's arm (which had been amputated that day) to Jane's room and slip it in her bed after she was asleep. They knew this would scare the living daylights out of Jane, but they thought perhaps it might force her to be nicer in the future.

The arm was carefully put in the bed with the sleeping Jane. The next morning she didn't come out. The nurses, thinking she might be unwell, went to investigate ...

They opened the door and saw Jane sitting on the bed. Her hair, black before, was now completely white, and she was gnawing on the arm, making gurgling noises and rocking. SHE HAD GONE COMPLETELY INSANE!

A young couple were parked in a remote spot when the music on the radio was interrupted by a news bulletin. A madman had escaped from the nearby asylum. He could be identified by the hook he had in place of his right hand. The girl wanted to be taken home immediately ... When they arrived at her house, the boy went over to open the car door for her ... and hanging from the handle was a BLOODY HOOK!

In Berlin after World War Two, money was short, food was in very short supply and everyone was hungry ...

A girl saw a blind man trying to cross the road. Being a kind soul, she helped him, and the two started to talk. He asked her for a favor: could she deliver a letter for him? The address on the envelope was on her way home, so she agreed. Left with the letter, she was about to go when she turned around to see the man hurrying away, suddenly without his dark glasses or his cane. She stopped a policeman and told him what had happened. He read the letter, and immediately called on three colleagues to hurry to the address. There, they found a slaughterhouse full of human flesh for sale.

The letter the girl had been given? It read: "THIS IS THE LAST ONE I AM SENDING YOU TODAY"

A woman and her boyfriend were on their way home one night, and suddenly his car ran out of gas. It was late, and they were alone in the middle of nowhere. The guy stepped out of the car, saying to his girlfriend, "Don't worry, lock the doors, I'll be right back with some help."

She locked the doors and waited. And waited. Suddenly, she noticed a shadow fall across her lap. She looked up to see, not her boyfriend, but a crazed-looking man. He was swinging something in his right hand. He stuck his face to the window of the locked door and slowly pulled up his right hand. In it was her boyfriend's head. The girl shut her eyes tightly in terror. When she dared to open them again, the man was still there, grinning psychotically.

He slowly lifted his left hand, and he was holding her boyfriend's keys–TO THE CAR!

Two girls were staying alone one stormy night in one of their homes, when suddenly, the power went out, plunging them into darkness.

While they lay in bed, they heard a noise. The braver of the girls put on her dressing gown – white, with a furry collar around the neck – and went downstairs to check what the sound was. Twenty minutes passed, and the girl upstairs in the dark got increasingly frightened. At last she heard feet coming down the hall, but she began to worry that it might not be her friend, but someone else ... She decided to hide behind the door with a lamp. When the person came in she would feel for the furry gown; if she couldn't feel it, she would lash out with the lamp.

The steps came closer. The door creaked open and the person was right next to her. She felt with her hand and found the fur collar. Feeling a little higher, all she felt was a STUMP where her friend's HEAD HAD BEEN!

As a woman was getting into her car, she noticed a man with a strange look on his face walking quickly towards her. She jumped into the car and drove away, but before long she saw the man was following her in another car. She panicked and drove home as quickly as she could, swerved into the driveway and screamed for her husband. Her husband ran out just as her pursuer pulled up, jumped from his car and yelled: "Lady, there's A MAN WITH A KNIFE HIDING IN YOUR BACK SEAT!"

A young woman returned to her car from a day's shopping. She had parked her car in a multi-story car park.
As she approached, she noticed someone sitting in the back seat. She checked the number plate to make sure it really was her car. It was, and she saw that the person in the back seat was an elderly woman. She asked the woman what she was doing.

The old woman replied that she had been shopping with her daughter, but felt unwell and returned to the car to rest. She'd obviously got the wrong car.

The old woman then asked to be taken to a hospital. The young woman, of course, agreed. As she got into the driver's seat she noticed her passenger's arms were very thick and hairy, and she started to feel uncomfortable with the whole situation.

She asked the old woman to get out of the car to direct her as she reversed it, and as soon as the old woman was out of the car, the young woman drove out of the car park, straight to the nearest police station where she reported the incident. A police officer then searched the young woman's car ... and found a bag tucked under the driver's seat. Inside the bag was a length of rope and a BLOOD-STAINED AXE.

MONSTROUS LUCK

You Win Some, You Lose Some

In 1981, depressed since he could not find a job, 42-year-old Romolo Ribolla sat in his kitchen near Pisa, Italy, with a gun in his hand threatening to end it all. His wife pleaded with him not to do it, and after about an hour he burst into tears and threw the gun to the floor, whereupon it went off and shot his wife dead.

Walter Hallas, a 26-year-old store clerk in Leeds, England, was so afraid of dentists that in 1979 he asked a friend to try to cure his toothache by knocking out the offending molar with a punch to the jaw. The punch caused him to fall down, hitting his head, and he died of a fractured skull.

A Spanish man doing some business in Poland one day came across a pretty church with a coffin inside laid out for viewing. No one else was there.

A little surprised, the businessman nevertheless said a prayer, and signed the book of condolences, leaving a note passing on good wishes on to the man's loved ones, and a business card. A month later he got a call from the dead man's lawyer.
It appears that the dead man had suspected that he could not trust his own family or business associates. He decided that only in death would he discover who, if anyone, cared for him, rather than just his money.

The deceased man's will stated that his multi-million dollar fortune was to be split evenly amongst all who attended his wake. The Spanish businessman was the only attendant, and inherited a massive fortune.

A family from England went on vacation to France, taking their wealthy and elderly grandma. She spent the entire trip moaning and grousing, until one day, she died.

They knew she would have wanted to be buried in England, but not wishing to spend days at customs on paperwork, they decided to hide her. They bought a cheap bit of carpet, rolled Granny up in it and strapped her on the roof. They drove back through France, through sunshine and rain, across the Channel by ferry, and made it through French and English customs without a hitch.

Having reached home, the family were devastated when, after a well-earned cup of tea, they went outside to find that the car had been stolen – carpet, Granny and all. They were never recovered, and being unable to produce a body, the family were unable to collect on the old lady's will.

A fierce gust of wind during a gale blew 45-year-old Vittorio Luise's car into a river near Naples, Italy, in 1983. He managed to break a window, climb out and swim to shore, where a tree blew over and killed him.

The Princess of Amen-Ra lived some 3,500 years ago. When she died, she was laid in an ornate wooden coffin and buried deep in a vault at Luxor, on the banks of the River Nile.

In the 1890s, four rich young Englishmen visiting the excavations at Luxor were invited to buy an exquisitely fashioned mummy case containing the remains of the Princess. They drew lots, and the man who won paid a lot of money and had the coffin taken to his hotel. Two hours later, he was seen walking into the desert. He never returned. The next day, one of the remaining men was accidentally shot by a servant.

The third man in the foursome found on his return home that his bank had gone out of business, leaving him penniless. The fourth man suffered a severe illness, lost his job and was reduced to selling matches in the street.

Nevertheless, the coffin reached England, where it was bought by a businessman. After three of his family had been injured in a road accident and his house damaged by fire, he donated the coffin to the British Museum.

As the coffin was being unloaded from a truck in the museum courtyard, the truck suddenly went into reverse and trapped a passer-by. Then, as the casket was being lifted up the stairs by two workmen, one fell and broke his leg. The other, apparently in perfect health, died unaccountably two days later.

Once the Princess was installed in the Egyptian Room, the trouble really started ...

The museum's nightwatchmen frequently heard hammering and sobbing from the coffin. Other exhibits in the room were often thrown about at night. Cleaners refused to go near the room. Finally, the authorities had the mummy carried to the basement. Within a week, the supervisor of the move was found dead at his desk.

The museum sold the mummy to a private collector. After suffering a miserable few years of illness and misfortune, the owner banished the coffin to the attic, where it remained until a hard-headed American archaeologist paid a handsome price for it and arranged for its removal and shipping to New York.

In April, 1912, the new owner escorted his treasure aboard a sparkling new White Star liner about to make its maiden voyage to New York. The name of the ship was, of course, the H.M.S. *Titanic*.

SOLD

Backways Cove is an isolated inlet just along the coast from the golden North Cornwall beach of Trebarwith Strand. It is said to be haunted, but no one really knows by whom: possibly the ghosts of shipwrecked sailors drowned when their vessels were torn apart on the treacherous rocks nearby, or maybe even the restless spirit of a local man doomed to haunt the scene of his crime – a crime with a curious twist in the tale.

Many years ago a man with two sons ran a large farm in the vicinity and, on his death, left his entire estate to his eldest son, cutting off the younger one without a penny. The younger son went away, jealous and confused at his father's actions. Convinced that he had been cheated of his birthright, he set out to take revenge on his elder brother. One night he returned to his childhood home, crept onto

the farm and set fire to the buildings. The entire property was burned to the ground. The ruins of this once prosperous farm may still be seen near Backways – a few stones from the farmhouse and outbuildings were all that remained after the fearsome blaze.

In the morning, the arsonist discovered that his brother had died the day before he had set the fire, and left the entire estate to him.

A man hit by a car in New York in 1977 got up uninjured, but lay back down in front of the car when a bystander told him to pretend he was hurt so he could collect the insurance money. The car then rolled forward and crushed him.

In 1983, a Mrs Carson of New York was laid out in her coffin, presumed dead of heart disease. As mourners watched, she suddenly sat up, alive as you or I. Unfortunately her daughter dropped dead of fright on the spot.

GRUESOME STORIES

Tales to Turn the Tummy

A couple had just moved into a small castle they'd recently purchased and were excitedly searching all the nooks and crannies. In a large underground room they found many empty barrels that had been drunk years ago, but one that appeared to be full. They immediately put a tap on it, and out poured a delicious brandy. They drank and served it at parties, enjoying not only its flavor, but the fact that it could have been hundreds of years old. Months later when the brandy stopped flowing, they noticed that the barrel was still too heavy to be empty. They cut it open with a saw, and found A SHRIVELLED CORPSE CURLED UP IN THE BOTTOM!

Tammi Wilder was a nice girl, but not too bright. One day she got asked on a date by one guy she really liked, so on the day of the date she wanted to look pretty.

The day came but Tammi never showed up. Days later her date decided to pay her a visit to find out why she'd stood him up. He went to her house, but there was no answer to his ringing on the bell. He went round the back of the house and looked in the kitchen window, only to see Tammi lying on the kitchen floor. The police reconstructed Tammi's last moments. The night of her date, she found her hair was still too wet to be combed, so an idea struck her. She would go to the kitchen, open the door of the microwave and falsely lock the door by pressing a knife up to the catch.

That way she could keep the door open and dry her hair inside the oven. Doctors diagnosed death by BOILED BRAIN!

"What is that red spot on my cheek?" young Ruth asked her mother one morning. "It looks like an insect bite," her mother said. "It will go away. Just don't scratch it."

Soon the small spot grew into a small boil. "Look at it now," Ruth said. "It's getting bigger. It's sore!" "That sometimes happens," her mother said. "It will calm down soon." In a few days the boil was even larger. "Look at it now," Ruth said. "It hurts and it's ugly!" "We'll have the doctor look at it tomorrow," her mother said. "Maybe it's infected."

That night Ruth took a hot bath. As she soaked herself, the boil burst, and out poured a swarm of tiny baby spiders from the eggs that had been laid in her cheek!

A man on a motorcycle was passing an eighteen-wheeled truck carrying sheet metal when one of the sheets shifted and fell off the side of the lorry, neatly cutting off the motorcyclist's head. His headless body continued on its route, overtaking the truck. The truck driver saw the headless biker overtaking and immediately had a heart attack, swerving his truck off the road into a ravine.

A motorcyclist was riding one winter, wearing his jacket backwards. This method made the jacket windproof and warm. He hit some ice and fell off his bike, and was unconscious but not seriously injured. A passing motorist saw the spill and leapt out of his car to help. Seeing the biker with the backwards jacket, he was horrified, assuming the crash had twisted the man's head 180 degrees! He felt fast action was vital, so he tried to twist the cyclist's head back to its proper position, BREAKING THE BIKER'S NECK!

A woman came home from shopping to find her Doberman dog choking on something. She quickly put him in the car and rushed him to the vet.

The vet told her to go home while he operated to remove whatever was lodged in the dog's windpipe, and he'd call her when she could pick up her pet.

The woman hadn't been home for long when the vet called and told her in an calm but urgent voice to get out of her house immediately, and that he'd come by to explain in a few minutes.

From her neighbor's window she saw the vet arrive with several police cars, and she ran out to see if her dog was all right and to see what was going on. As the police ran into her house, the vet told her what her loving pet had choked on:

TWO HUMAN FINGERS! The police found an escaped maniac hiding in the wardrobe nursing his mangled hand!

Henry Page's wife became deathly ill the night before Christmas in 1798. He called for the doctor, but by the time the doctor arrived the woman had died, or so it seemed. Her husband was so grief-stricken that he shut himself up on his own and didn't attend the funeral the following day.

The servants of the house carried the woman's body to the local minister, who held a ceremony quickly. A veil was drawn over her face, and a stone lid lowered on her casket. Later that night, the clergyman was drifting to sleep, when he suddenly remembered the beautiful emerald ring the woman had been wearing on her finger ...

He went downstairs, lifted the lid and tried to pry off the ring. It wouldn't budge. So he fetched a knife, severed her finger and pulled off the ring. As he left, he turned around to pick up the casket lid and screamed at the top of his voice, dropped the ring and ran. The woman had awakened and was moaning and holding her severed finger towards him with a look of horror on her face!

The churchman turned tail and ran, never to return. He didn't realize that the woman was only trying to thank him, for she had not died after all, but had gone into a coma, and the man's treachery had woken her.

Wearing nothing but her fine silk dress, she walked back to her home, but could rouse no one. The servants had all gone to sleep for it was late on Christmas Eve. She lifted up a heavy stone and heaved it at her husband's window, smashing it. He came to the window with a sorrowful look on his face, and suddenly to her surprise he yelled out: "Go away! Don't you know my wife has died. Leave me in peace to mourn her and do not bother me again!"

She shouted back, "I am your so-called dead wife! Now come down here and open this door, Henry Page, unless you'd like me to die a second time on our doorstep!" Delirious with joy, Henry Page came down to meet his wife and took her inside.

They both lived long lives and their first son was born the following spring.

A college girl was getting ready for a party and decided she needed a tan. She spent Thursday and Friday going from salon to salon, only leaving when the management refused to let her stay any longer for safety reasons. She finally achieved the color she wanted and went out Friday night. The next morning, her horrified housemates found her in bed, dead.

An autopsy on the body revealed that SHE HAD LITERALLY COOKED HER INSIDES!

A young couple purchased a new mattress for their bed, but when it arrived it seemed lumpy, and, on waking after a couple of nights, the wife discovered scratches on her neck and body, and felt queasy and faint.

She was taken straight to the local hospital, where she made a complete recovery, though even after examination doctors were still mystified as to the cause of her injuries. The couple decided after a few days that their new mattress was just awful and returned it to the retailer. The store couldn't figure out why it was so lumpy so they took the mattress apart to look for any faults in its construction.

They discovered that during the manufacture of the mattress in South America, a huge anaconda had snuck into the half-finished mattress and had been accidentally sewn into it. The snake was still alive, and the couple had been SLEEPING ON IT FOR THREE DAYS!

IT'S A MYSTERY

Curiouser and Curiouser

When two motorists were found dead in their undamaged cars a short distance apart on a German road, police were mystified. After a lengthy forensic examination, the story was eventually revealed. The two motorists were driving in heavy fog. Each was guiding his car carefully at a snail's pace near the middle of the road. At the moment of impact their heads were both out of the driver's side windows when they cracked together, leaving the unmarked cars to roll gently to a halt 200 yards apart.

A man and a woman happened to sit next to one another on a train. The woman took out a book and began reading. The train stopped at half a dozen stations, but she never looked up once. The man watched her for a while, then asked, "What are you reading?"

"A ghost story," she said. "It's very good. Very spooky."

"Do you believe in ghosts?" he asked.

"Yes, I do," she replied. "There are ghosts everywhere."

"I don't believe in them," he said. "It's just a lot of superstition. In all my years, I've never seen a ghost, not one."

"Haven't you?" the woman said, and vanished.

One morning in 1954, Sven James Thoresen found himself walking along a street in his home town. He could not explain what he was doing there, or remember how he got there, or where he had been earlier. He didn't even know what time it was. He saw a woman walking towards him and stopped her.

"I've forgotten my watch," he said. "Can you tell me the time?"

When she saw him, she screamed and ran away. Other people seemed afraid of him too. When they saw him, they looked aghast, flattened themselves against buildings, or ran across the street! "There must be something wrong with me," Sven thought. "I'd better get home."

He flagged down a taxi, but the driver took one look at him and sped off. "This is crazy!" he thought to himself. He was confused and frightened. He found a public telephone and called home, expecting his wife's voice. Instead, a strange voice answered.

"Is Mrs Thoresen there?" he asked. "I'm sorry, she isn't," the voice said. "Her husband died a few days ago in a horrible car crash. She's at his funeral."

GHOSTLY GOINGS ON

That's the Spirit!

In southwest England stands Longleat House. In the 18th century, the second Viscount, Thomas, lived there and married one Louisa Carteret. Local legend had it that he suspected her of having an affair with a footman and murdered him with the help of two servants, hiding the body.

Louisa died not long after – of a broken heart, they said. The Viscount started to see her ghost, smell her perfume, and see things move on their own. He fled the house in fear and never returned. Three centuries later, workmen dug up some flagstones outside the house and found a man's corpse dressed in 18th-century clothes.

They buried him in a graveyard not far from the house, near the tomb of Thomas: murderer and victim together for all eternity. "The Grey Lady of Louisa", as she became known, still haunts the house to this day.

In the year 1910, a young Frenchwoman on her way to a shopping trip in Paris broke her journey by staying at an old manor house hotel ...

... late that night, she heard the noise of horses' hooves on the gravel outside. She got up and went over to the window. The moonlight was very bright, and she saw a horse-drawn hearse drive up to the door. It didn't have a coffin in it, but it was crowded to bursting point with people.

As the coachman came by the window, he turned his head to the girl and said in a low growl, "There's room for one more ..."

The frightened girl drew the curtains, ran back to bed, and covered her head with the bedclothes. In the morning she wasn't sure whether it had been a dream, or whether she had really seen the hearse, but she was glad to leave the hotel.

In Paris, she was shopping in a big store with a large elevator in it – a novelty at that time. She was on the top floor, and went to the elevator to go down. It was crowded, and as she came up to it, the elevator operator turned his head and said, "There's room for one more." It was the face of the hearse coachman. "No, thank you," said the girl. "I'll walk down." She turned away; the elevator doors clanged shut; there was a terrible rush, and screaming and shouting, and then a great clatter and huge crash. The elevator had fallen, and everybody in it was killed.

In 1922, Robert Townsend went to a party with some of his friends. At that party he met the prettiest girl that he had ever seen. Millie had long brown hair and eyes like emeralds. He asked her to dance and she seemed pleased to accept. Later, he walked her home. It was raining, and she borrowed his coat. They kissed. The next day, he returned to the house for his jacket. A grey-haired woman answered. He asked after Millie, and the lady wept. "I'm sorry," she said, "my daughter died a year ago today." Robert gasped. "But I just saw her yesterday!" The lady said, "Go to the cemetery a mile down the road, and you'll find her there."

Robert found the cemetery. He searched for the girl's grave, and found one with her name on it. Lying there was his jacket. When he picked it up, a note fell to the ground. It read: "I'M SORRY, MY LOVE."

One of the most famous ghosts in the southern states of the USA is "Soap Sally". In the 1950s, there was an old lady soap-maker who walked the streets of the mill villages kidnapping children and murdering them to use the fat in their bodies to make soap. There were numerous reports of people having seen her for years after her death. Every time a child went missing, Soap Sally could be seen wandering the streets, carrying her knapsack full of soap.

In the mid-western states of America around a hundred years ago, two gentlemen were working in a town's small general store. A small frail woman dressed in grey entered the shop, picked up a glass container of milk and, without paying for it or even glancing at the gentlemen, walked out ...

... the men, surprised by the woman's thievery, hurried out of the store after her,

but she had disappeared. A few days later, the incident occurred again, and a few weeks later, a third time. The men, slightly more prepared, followed the woman out of the store, down the town's main street and down a path that led to a cemetery neither of them knew existed. Suddenly, they heard a noise, which they identified as a baby's cry. It was coming from the under the ground in front of a gravestone marking the death of a mother and her baby who were buried together. Unsure of what else to do, the men quickly found shovels and dug up the coffin. The crying became louder as they dug. When they reached the coffin, they pried off the lid and inside found the woman – dead – with a live, crying baby in her arms, and three empty glass milk containers. The poor child was mistakenly buried alive and the spirit of her deceased mother had kept her alive until she was found.

Once there was a little girl, Amy, whose grandfather had just died. She had loved him very much and missed him terribly. He was buried in a cemetery just a few hundred yards from her house, and she could see his grave from her bedroom window.

One night, her parents were going out and the babysitter hadn't arrived. She was a very reliable sitter, so, trusting she would soon arrive, they kissed Amy goodbye and left. Hours passed and the babysitter had still not arrived. Amy began to worry. A storm was brewing outside. Thunder and lightning moved closer to the house and the wind started howling. Suddenly there was a flash of lightning and the power in the house went off, leaving Amy in darkness. The wind ripped the trees around and branches broke off, crashing against the house and falling to the ground. Alone in the dark, Amy was very scared.

Suddenly, the phone rang. She answered, hoping it was her parents or the sitter. Sounding far away, a voice came over the phone: it belonged to her grandfather. "Don't be afraid, honey. There's nothing to fear. You'll be safe. The storm will pass."
Then the phone went silent.

Amy went to bed happy, and slept well in spite of the raging storm outside. Her parents came home to find her sound asleep. They were horrified when the babysitter called the next morning to explain that her car had been blown into a ditch in the storm. When they woke Amy, she told them what had happened. They had a hard time believing her, but she smiled and pointed out of the window.

The phone line from the house was intact to the first pole, but then it had snapped. The cable drooped into the cemetery where its end lay across her grandfather's grave.

A young couple moved in to a new home in Hawaii. They had a young son, Bobby, whom they would put to bed each night, only to find him the next morning sleeping on the floor in the corner of his room ...

... One day, the father put a wardrobe in that corner, and that night while the couple was watching TV, they turned to see their son walking out of his room as if he was holding someone's hand. Just before he got to the door, he dropped his hand as if the person had let go. He woke up crying. The couple were scared, and they called upon a Hawaiian priest for help. He told them that their house was built on a "night marching trail" – a path taken by ghosts. The priest said Bobby always slept in a corner because a friendly spirit had put him there for safety, to keep him away from the ghosts, who might have taken him on their march, never to be seen again.

A massive ghost hunt organized by Dr Richard Wiseman of Hertfordshire University in England earned a place in the *Guinness Book of World Records*. The search for spirits took place in April 2000, in underground vaults beneath the streets of Edinburgh, Scotland. Two hundred and fifty people and dozens of high-tech sensors were employed in the search of the tombs. Despite the record-breaking effort, not a single ghost was sighted, or heard.

The ghost of Abraham Lincoln is probably the most active of departed famous people. Assassinated in 1865, Lincoln lives on in the White House, according to a number of witnesses who claim to have heard and even seen the 16th president at 1600 Pennsylvania Avenue.

A young clerk in the Roosevelt administration claimed to have seen the

ghost of Lincoln sitting on a bed and pulling off his boots ... and while spending a night at the White House during the Roosevelt presidency, Queen Wilhelmina of the Netherlands was awakened by a knock on the bedroom door. Answering it, she was faced with the ghost of Abe Lincoln staring at her from the hallway.

During one of Winston Churchill's visits to the United States during World War Two, he spent the night in the White House. Churchill loved to retire late and take a long, hot bath with a glass of scotch and a cigar. On this occasion, he climbed out of the bath, naked but for his cigar, and walked into the bedroom. He was startled to see Abraham Lincoln standing by the fireplace in the room, leaning on the mantle. Churchill blinked and said, "Good evening, Mr. President. You seem to have me at a disadvantage." Lincoln smiled softly and disappeared.

Two centuries ago, the military post at Fort Union in wild New Mexico was the only spot for miles around where any kind of social life could be found.

The young sister-in-law of a captain enjoyed the attention the young officers paid to her, flirting, dancing and enjoying her position as one of the few single young ladies in camp. A lieutenant fell for her, and hoped he might win her hand, but was put in command of a patrol to fight an Apache force nearby.

Before he left, he confided his love to the lady, who promised that if he were not to return she would never marry another. In a few days the detachment came back, but the lieutenant was missing.

His bride-to-be seemed to forget him quickly, and nobody was surprised when she soon announced her marriage to a wealthy young

man from New York. As the wedding dance was in full swing, a door flew open with a crash and a cry echoed through the place. All eyes turned to the door. In it stood a man in a blood-stained officer's uniform, his head marked by a hatchet-gash, his scalp gone, his eyes burning with a terrible light.
The officer drew her from the arms of her husband, who stood frozen as in a trance, and, clasping her to him, began a waltz.
The couple spun around and around, the girl growing paler and paler, until at last her fallen jaw and staring eyes declared that the life had been drained from her body. The soldier let her sink to the floor and stood over her, wringing his hands and moaning, before vanishing through the door whence he came.

The following day, a troop of soldiers visited the scene of the Apache encounter and returned with the body of the missing lieutenant. He'd been dead for three months.

MURDER MOST FOUL

Corpses and Killers

Robert Louis Stevenson's tale of Dr Jekyll & Mr Hyde may well have been inspired by a man called William Brodie. By day, he was a respected man of society and Deacon of Edinburgh. At night, he frequented the dark parts of the town, committing gruesome murders. He was caught and sentenced to hang for his crimes, but before visiting the gallows, he slipped a metal tube in his throat to prevent his neck from snapping. After the hanging, his body was cut from the gallows and returned to his house by friends, where a private doctor was on hand to attempt to revive him. When later his coffin was re-opened following rumors of his trick, his corpse had vanished.

In 1948, Edith Wills was travelling one night alone on the London Underground. She sat opposite three people in an otherwise empty carriage. She settled down and looked up. The woman opposite was staring at her. Edith got out her book and started to read but every time she looked up, she caught the woman's gaze. The train pulled into a station and an elderly man got on and sat next to her. As the train pulled out, he leaned back and said in her ear, "If you know what's good for you, you'll get off at the next station with me." Edith was scared but decided to get off anyway, hoping that there might be people around.

She left the train with the elderly man at the next stop. The man said "I didn't mean to scare you, but I'm a doctor. The woman sitting opposite you was quite clearly dead. The men either side were holding her up."

Lisa's parents had gone to a party for the evening. And all poor Lisa had to do was stay home and watch her two little brothers.

She was making pasta when the phone rang. Lisa answered. "I'm near," said a woman's voice. "Near where?" Lisa replied, but the other end was dead. A little shaken, Lisa checked on the kids and finished cooking. After dinner, she put the kids to bed, turned on the TV, and was flicking through the channels when the phone rang again …
She ran to the phone before it woke the kids. "I'm closer," said the woman on the other end. "Excuse me?" said Lisa. But again, silence.

She called the operator. "I'm getting strange calls here and I was wondering if you can tell me where they came from?" she asked.

"No," replied the operator, "but I can put a tap on your line and trace any further calls …"

Lisa woke up the boys. The phone rang. She told the kids to be quiet and answered. The woman's voice said, "I'm here now, and my, it is so sharp ..." She giggled. "Huh? Wh–What's so sharp?" Lisa blurted. "Where are you?" But the woman hung up.

Instantly the phone rang again. It was the operator. "Get out now! Those calls are coming from inside your house!"

Lisa slammed down the phone, grabbed her keys and the kids and flew out of the front door. They got in the car and locked all the doors. Police cars came roaring up the driveway. They searched everywhere until they finally came to the attic ...

... there they found a middle-aged woman with wild hair and eyes sitting with a mobile phone and a butcher's knife, dribbling as she sharpened it on a stone.

MONSTER GAMES!

Pass the Parcel Forfeits

Get a prize and wrap it up. Put as many layers of wrapping on it as you want but make sure each layer is wrapped individually. As you wrap each layer, put a sticker on it with instructions for the player to follow, such as "Scream", "Do an impression of a bat", "Swap shoes with the person on your left", "Draw a skull and crossbones on your own forehead", etc. To start the game, everyone sits in a circle, one person controlling the music. Once the music starts, you must pass the parcel around the circle, making sure everyone in the circle gets to pass it on to the next person. When the music stops, the person who has the parcel must unwrap just one layer, read the instructions and carry them out, and the person who unwraps the prize, wins it!

Shrunken Head Polo

Draw a scary face on a couple of oranges: these are the "shrunken heads".

Then get two pairs of tights and put another orange in one foot of each of them.
Each player ties the empty tights leg round their waist so the orange hangs down between their legs: this is your polo mallet.
You must swing it between your legs to hit the shrunken head on the floor.
Players split into two teams, and the game is played as a relay.
Each player knocks the shrunken head up and down a course before passing the tights to the next player. The first team to finish, wins!

Stomp Head
Divide the group into two teams. Tie a balloon to each player's ankle: red for one team, blue for another, and draw scary faces on the balloons for added halloweenyness. Say "Go!" and watch the teams trying to burst the other team's balloons first. As your balloon is burst you have to leave the game, and the team with the last unpopped balloon wins!

Autopsy

Make an outline of a body on the ground and place various fruits and veggies within the outline to look like body organs. You can use almost anything for the parts: a cauliflower for the brain, a ripe, peeled tomato for the heart, cold spaghetti for the guts, carrots and celery for bones, grapes for eyeballs, jelly for the kidneys, etc. Then place a very large black plastic bag over the outline and cut hand-size holes in it to allow players to feel the "body parts"!

Pumpkinhead

Like an egg and spoon race, but each person puts a pumpkin on his or her head. When the whistle is blown, you go as quickly as you can towards the finish line. Whoever makes it there first – without the pumpkin falling off their head – wins. If the pumpkin falls off, you're out, and no touching the pumpkin with your hands!

Halloween Murder

Everyone stands in a circle. The lights are turned off. Everyone closes their eyes; one person, who isn't in this round, walks around the circle and taps the person of their choice on the shoulder. No one is to know who that person is. Now the lights are turned back on. Everyone shakes everyone else's hand, and the person who was tapped on the shoulder (the murderer!) will tickle one person's palm with his index finger. The tickled person must then count to ten (so that the murderer can move away). After ten seconds the person who was tickled falls to the floor, pretending to be dead. Now everyone must try to guess who did it (one guess each). If the murderer gets away with it, he or she wins and gets to pick the next murderer. If someone guesses correctly who the killer is, they win, and get to choose the next murderer.

Team Scarecrows

This game needs two teams and two bags of identical clothing items: a scarf, hat, gloves, jumper, jacket, trousers and sunglasses. Each team chooses one person to be the scarecrow. It's a relay, each person taking a turn reaching into a bag filled with clothing and running to the scarecrow to put it on him or her. As soon as the scarecrow has the article of clothing completely on, that person runs back to tag the next person to get something from the bag. The first team to have all the articles of clothing on the scarecrow is the winner!

Guts Fishing

Place five or more marbles in a big bowl, bucket or pan. Fill it with cold cooked spaghetti, ketchup and a little oil. Players must root through the mixture with bare feet and attempt to find an "eyeball". Each player gets thirty seconds!

Tarantula

Get some wool and cut a number of small pieces. Put a piece of tape on one end of each piece and tie a number to the other end. Criss-cross the pieces of yarn all over a room to create a big "web". Each player grabs a taped end of yarn and rolls it up until they get to the numbers. Each number corresponds to a special treat, with a prize for the first player to find their number!

Body Part Relay

Make up a skeleton's bones with cut-out card. Hide the parts throughout the room. Team members must run around the room and find all their parts and reassemble their skeleton. This can be done one team at a time with the fastest team winning. Or, teams can compete simultaneously, with each team having their parts of the skeleton hidden in a different side of the room.

Spooky Stories

You need different colored pieces of card, one for each of the categories described on the opposite page. Write these words on cut-out pieces of card so that you have four well-shuffled decks of cards, face down.

The first player takes a card from the "Ghouls" pile, and starts to tell a story about the character named on the card, stopping after ten to thirty seconds. Then it is the next player's turn.

This player draws a card from the "Beasts" pile and continues the story, and must include the word on this card. The next player must pick a card from the "Stuff" pile, weaving it into the tale, and the player after that draws from the ""Sound effects" pile, and must add it to the tale. Storytelling continues until someone pulls a "The End" card.

The player who draws this card must end the story in the best way they can!

Categories for Spooky Stories

GHOULS	BEASTS	STUFF	SOUND EFFECTS
Ghost	Black cat	Broomstick	Boo!
Witch	Bat	Cauldron	Whap!
Skeleton	Rat	Coffin	Squeeek
Mummy	Spider	Fire	Ahhhhh!
Frankenstein	Shark	Magic Wand	Bang!
Vampire	Raven	Pumpkin	Shhhh!
Princess	Owl	Silver bullet	Clump. . .clump
Werewolf	Wolf	Sword	Arrrrgh!
Invisible Man	Dog	Treasure chest	Craaaaash!
Alien	Tiger	Wooden stake	Scratch-scratch
Zombie	Fly	Apples	EEEEK!!!
Psychopath	Toad	Jack-o-lantern	Thump!!
Yeti	Snake	Spell book	Creeeeek!
Weird child	Scorpion	Laser	Pop!
Wizard	Jackal	Torch	Achoo!!
Quasimodo	Dragon	Poison	Ooh-la-la!
Robber	Vulture	Machine gun	Whoosh!
Monster	Hyena	Corpse	Ow!
Stranger	Moth	Skull	Crunch!
The End	The End	The End	The End

Murder Circle

Each player draws a piece of paper from a hat. Each piece of paper bears the word "Victim" except for one marked "Murderer". All players must sit in a circle so they can see all the other players' faces. The Murderer tries to "kill" the other players by winking at them, without the other players seeing them do it. If a player is winked at, he or she must "die" loudly and stay dead. Any "live" player who thinks they know who the killer is, shouts "Detective!" and guesses the murderer's identity. If they are right, they win; if they are wrong, they too are "dead"! The murderer wins if all but one "Victim" is killed off without being detected. "Victims" are not allowed to wink!

The Wizard's Cauldron

Get five different kinds of drinks (milk, orange juice, cola, etc) and 20 or so bowls of different foods (grapes, chocolate, cheese, cornflakes, broken biscuits, etc.) Each player is blindfolded and spun around. They must choose two drinks and three food items by pointing at them. Other players then make up a little cocktail in a paper cup from the items the player has picked, and he or she must drink it! The winner is the player who can correctly identify the five ingredients. (Keep a bucket handy – this can be disgusting!)

Pumpkin Plastic Surgeon

Three teams, three pumpkins. Carve a face into each pumpkin, saving the pieces that make up the eyes, nose, and mouth. Mix up these pieces from the different pumpkins in one bowl. Each team sends one person at a time to get a piece to take back to their assigned pumpkin. If the piece of pumpkin they choose fits, then the next person on their team can go to the table, otherwise they have to go back and get another piece. The game is over when the first team has all the right parts!

Witch Hunt

Make a witch pattern on a piece of paper, then make 50 or more out of black paper and hide them all over your house and garden. Split the party into teams of two or three and say "Go!" The team that comes back with the most witches in 20 minutes, wins!

Pass the Brains

A Halloween variation of "pass the parcel". Scoop out a pumpkin as you would to make a jack-o-lantern. Carve out a face, but don't make the holes too big otherwise the "brains" will fall out. Fill the pumpkin with cold, cooked spaghetti, hiding wrapped sweets in amongst the "brains". There should be one sweet for each child playing. Play some spooky music as the pumpkin head is passed around. When the music stops, the child holding the head feels through its "brains" to find a sweet. Messy but fun!

Eyeball Suckers

Float lots of marshmallow "eyeballs" in a bucket of water. Each player gets a straw and must grab as many eyeballs as they can by sucking them onto the straw and putting them on a paper plate in front of them. The player with the most eyeballs when they have all been sucked up, wins!

Goobubble

Cover pieces of bubblegum on a paper plate with green instant pudding, one for each player. Put the plates on the floor. The first player to dive in, hands behind back, find the bubblegum and blow a bubble is the winner!

Making Mummies

You need an even number of people and a lot of toilet paper. Get everybody into pairs. The object of the game is to see which pair can wrap each other up as mummies the fastest!

Witch Bogies

Draw a life-sized picture of a witch, with a big nose, and stick it on a door. Give each player chewing gum, and let them chew for a couple of minutes. One at a time, blindfold each player and spin them around.

Tell them to take the gum out of their mouth, and stick the "bogie" to the end of the witch's nose. Closest player wins!

Musical Headstones

Each player gets a "headstone" made of card or paper with some appropriate wording ("Rest in Peace", "Dearly Departed", etc.) written on it. Put the stones in a circle on the floor. Each player lies down with their head on a stone. When the music starts, everyone stands up and walks around the circle zombie-style. While they are walking, one stone is removed, and when the music stops, the players must jump into their "graves". The player without a headstone is eliminated. Continue until there is a winner!

Blindfold Executioner

Each player is given a piece of paper and a pencil and is blindfolded. The Game Master tells everyone to draw the base of a gallows, then the post, crossbar, rope, victim's head, body, arms and legs. Artists must remove their hand from the paper between drawing the different parts. The winner is the artist whose drawing looks the least weird!

Blind Man's Stumps

Blindfold one person and put a wooden spoon in each of his or her hands. Then spin the person around a few times while everyone moves around the room. Then everyone must freeze, and the "Blind Man" tries to find someone. When he does, he feels around the shape of the person who is caught using only his "stumps". The person has three guesses to figure out whom he has caught. If he guesses right, then the other person becomes the next Blind Man!

Head Chucking

You'll need lots of balloons with scary faces drawn on them, filled with water and air. Put the players into pairs and give each pair a beach towel to hold flat between them. One team begins by placing a water balloon in the middle of their towel. The object of the game is to toss the water balloon over a net, with the opposing team catching the balloon in their towel. The game continues until one side misses and the balloon bursts, giving them a soaking and the other team a point!

As soon as a team has dropped a balloon, they are replaced with a fresh team. The team with the most points when you run out of balloons are the champions! Beware, everyone will get wet playing this game!

With all balloon games, take care to dispose of popped balloons. They can be a choking hazard for young children.

Fishing for Nasties

Fill a bucket with water and split everyone into teams of three or so. Each team is blindfolded and must identify three objects you have previously placed in the bucket. Try bananas covered in jam, a sock full of jelly, a small cuddly toy, a bag of grapes, or anything else that feels nasty when wet! Members of a team all get to feel the object. The team that identifies all three of their items quickest, wins!

Murder in the Dark

From a deck of cards, take one card for each player, including just one ace, one jack, and one queen. Shuffle these cards and pass one out to each person. The person who gets the ace is the Detective, and they must leave the room for a minute. The person who gets the jack is the Murderer, and the person with the queen is the Victim. All others are innocent bystanders ... *(Continued on next page.)*

The players in the room after the Detective leaves must quietly find out who has the jack and queen. The Murderer "kills" the Victim, and the Victim must scream! The Victim's scream is the cue for the Detective to enter and begin his investigations.

The Detective is going to ask each person for an alibi, including the Murderer. The Detective will ask each person three times. The second and third times around the Murderer has to change one word in his or her story. For example, the Murderer might say, "I was swimming at the pool with Jack" the first time, "I went swimming at the pool with Jack" the second time, and lastly, "I went swimming to the pool with Jack." The Detective must try to figure out who the Murderer is, and if he guesses right, the Detective wins. If he doesn't, the Murderer wins!

Monster's Bad Day

The players sit in a circle. The first player starts by saying, "Monster got up in the morning and banged his head on a cupboard door." The next player must repeat "Monster got up in the morning and banged his head on a cupboard door," and add another misfortune, like "Then he dropped his bowl of cereal" or "Then he went outside and got run over by a bus." This continues all the way around the circle with each player reciting the accidents in the exact order they have been given and then adding a new one. If a player makes a mistake he or she drops out of the circle and the game continues. The last person to recite perfectly the Monster's Bad Day wins!

Bobbing for Spam

This is exactly like bobbing for apples, except you need a larger tub and you are bobbing for a whole Spam (taken out of the tin, naturally). The spam doesn't behave quite like an apple – it's slimy and it tends to fall to pieces after a while. In fact it's a messy, gross, disgusting game that is absolutely perfect for Halloween!

Pinata

A big tradition in Central and South America. A pinata is usually made of papier mâché (cover a balloon with papier mâché and let it dry). Paint the pinata like a skull or a scary pumpkin face, make a small hole in the top and fill it with sweets and gifts. Then hang it from a tree. The kids are blindfolded and given a stick and must try to smash the pinata with it. The kid that successfully breaks the pinata and makes the sweets rain down wins a special prize!

Monster Racing

Each "Monster" is two people joined at the legs by wearing a pair of tights (each sharing one of the legs) and at the upper body by sharing a big jumper, with one arm each. Make an obstacle race with blankets to crawl under and hoops to jump into, and race the Monsters in pairs until you get a winner!

Death of Dracula

Players form a circle round a blindfolded player. This middle player is Doctor Van Helsing, and he is equipped with a long balloon (his "stake"). The players in a circle must move around Van Helsing until he stays "Stop, Dracula!" When he say this, the players stop moving and Van Helsing stabs forward with his "stake". The player hit by the balloon must (in a disguised voice) say "Curses, Van Helsing, Aaaaaargh!" The blindfolded Van Helsing must then try to guess whom he has staked. If he gets it right, Dracula becomes the next Van Helsing. If he gets it wrong, he has to start again!

Doctor Frankenstein

Cut out and paint a Frankenstein's monster from an unfolded cardboard box. Cut holes where his brain, heart, liver and kidneys go. Split everyone into two teams and arm the teams with beanbags, ping pong balls or whatever's handy to represent the missing organs. From a distance of around ten feet, the fastest team to throw an organ into all four body cavities is the winner!

Pass the Guts

Players are split into two teams and line up. At one end of each line is a bowl of cold cooked spaghetti with tomato sauce. At the other end is an empty bowl. On the word "go", each team must pass their "guts" along the line to the bowl at the other end.

Players may use only one hand! The team that successfully gets all its guts into the finishing bowl is the winner! Beware, this is a very messy game!

Who Am I?

When the children come through the door, tape a drawing of a scary character to their backs (a ghost, monster, skeleton, bat, witch, etc.) They can ask anyone questions as to which character they are, but only questions that can have a "yes" or "no" answer. As soon as they have successfully guessed what creature they are representing, they must go to the host of the party and do an impression of it to receive their prize!

Pin the Stake on Dracula

Cut out a large Dracula shape from card or paper, draw in the face and clothes and put an "X" where his heart should be. Hang Dracula on the wall. Blindfold all players and give them a red pen. Turn the player around three times and have each player put a dot on Dracula and write their name next to it. The player that comes nearest Dracula's heart, wins!

DV

Raspberry Racing

Every player gets an uninflated balloon, which they personalize with a scary face and their name before blowing it up, but without tying a knot in it. Place a marker on the floor about 20 feet from the players. Each player then lets their balloon go splurting through the air, with the player whose balloon gets closest to the marker being declared the winner!

Monster Racing 2

Make two pairs of Monster Shoes by taping an old pair of shoes securely to a couple of old telephone directories. Complete the monster racing kit with heavy cardboard tubes which fit like stiff sleeves on the monsters so they can't bend their arms. Split all the players into two teams. The object of the race is to get water from a bucket at the end of the garden into your team cup at the other end with a ladle or a

big spoon. Taking turns, each racer must don the monster shoes and arms, galumph down the garden to the bucket, put the ladle in and carry as much water as he can back to his team's cup without spilling it. The team that fills the cup first is the winner. Only monsters in costume can touch the ladle!

Vampire Relay

You'll need a bowl of peas and some drinking straws for this one. Split everyone into two teams and give everyone (the Vampires) a cut-in-half drinking straw to use as fangs. On the command "go", one Vampire from each team must run to the bowl of peas and – using his fangs only – pick up two peas from the bowl using suction. The Vampires then run back to their team, drop the peas in a team cup and the next Vampire can go. The team who, at the final whistle, has the most peas in their cup is the winner! Any peas dropped on the way back from the bowl don't count!

Write your own monster jokes or stories here!

Draw your own monsters here!